CHAPTERS

FROM

CHILDHOOD

CHAPTERS

FROM

CHILDHOOD

Reminiscences of an Artist's Granddaughter

JULIET M. SOSKICE

TURTLE POINT PRESS

First published in 1921 in Great Britain
by Selwyn & Blount, Ltd.

© 1994 Turtle Point Press

Library of Congress Catalog Card Number: 93-061589

Design and composition by Wilsted & Taylor

Printed in the U.S.A.

Cover illustration: *The Artist's Daughter Louise, 1874.*
Albert Anker. The Oskar Reinhart Foundation.
Winterthur, Switzerland

Contents

❖

CHAPTER ONE

Social Reformers

For some time after my father's death my mother was ill and away, and I was sent to live with my aunt and uncle.*
They lived in a large grey house with steps up to the front door, and steps down to the area, and a great many stairs leading up to the top landings. The walls of all the rooms and staircases were covered with pictures, many with very bright colours in broad gilt frames. There were some portraits of other relations painted by a famous artist who was my uncle's brother.†

I had four cousins, who, though they were young, were social reformers. Mary was seven; Helen was nine; Arthur was about fourteen; and Olive was fifteen at least. I was eight, and I became a social reformer too.

*Mr. and Mrs. William Michael Rossetti.
†Dante Gabriel Rossetti.

We were anarchists. We believed that all people should be equal, and that nobody should possess more than anybody else; and we hoped for the social revolution. We had one big red banner in common, and we three little ones had a smaller one of the same colour for our special use. They both had some words on them, cut out of silver paper and pasted on with glue. I don't remember the words, but they were mottoes of some kind. The banners looked very bright and expensive, especially in the open air.

We had an anarchist page-boy. He was the son of my aunt's French cook. He had red hair and a cross, spotty face, and he used to open the door in the afternoon when visitors came. When he wasn't sitting in the hall he was supposed to be helping his mother in the kitchen, peeling potatoes and cleaning boots. But he never seemed to do much work. He disliked work because it tired him so. When he was in the kitchen he used to sit by the table with his arms spread out upon it and eat whatever his mother put in front of him, and when she would not give him any more he went into the larder to find food. He never said what he was going to eat, so that we were always being disappointed at table because at the last moment he had eaten something that was needed in the cooking. At first his mother used to say it was the cat, but after a time it couldn't be hidden any longer, because he ate so many things no cat would ever touch. He sulked

2

when he was spoken to about it, and grumbled because he had not been educated to be a public speaker.

He, of course, also thought that everybody should be equal and possess no more than everybody else. He said that he, for instance, was a uniformed slave of the capitalist system. He used to lie on the dining-room sofa with his legs thrown up over the back of it and his coat unbuttoned and explain his views about it. He thought it was a shame that he was forced to wear a coat with a long row of degrading buttons up the front as a token of servitude, and waste his youth on helping his mother who toiled and sweated in our kitchens while we, the representatives of the tyrant classes, wore what we liked and were provided for.

He said that he was a son of France, and that in France they had once got up a revolution and chopped the heads off all the tyrants. Tyrants' heads rolled off into the basket underneath the guillotine as quickly as peas out of the shucks into the basin when his mother shelled them. One day, he said, the same thing would happen here, and then "*our*" turn would come, and he and his mother and their kind would triumph. Till then they would be patient and hug their grief in secret. French people are more excitable and say more serious things than the English do. We used to sit round him on the floor, and hug our knees and listen. We felt ashamed and apologetic, and it was very difficult to think of anything to say to comfort him. Of course, it wasn't our fault, and we longed for the revolution. It was in our programme. Once my aunt came in and found him lying on the sofa, and she grabbed him by the ear and led him straight out of the room, right to the top of the kitchen stairs. She said she only kept him for his mother's sake. We all got up from the floor and stood close together. I shall never forget how angry we were, and how terrible our faces looked when she was doing it. It seemed to come just as a proof of what he was always saying: how unjust the world was, and how the tyrants always got the best of it.

We had an anarchist printing press down in the front room of the basement. We printed an anarchist newspaper on it. Olive and Arthur wrote most of the articles themselves. The page always promised to write something for it, but he never did, because he said he couldn't find the time. Sometimes they got an article from a real outside social reformer. The paper was called *The Torch*, and we used to sell it in Hyde Park on Sunday, and on the platforms of the biggest railway stations. I think it must have been interesting and uncommon, because whenever anybody bought a copy they would first stand for some time staring at the cover, and as soon as they got to the title of the first article they would to an absolute certainty (we knew because we used to watch) turn round suddenly and stare after us. I can't remember the headings of any of the articles, but I think there was an incitement to revolution in every copy. It was probably most about the moans of the classes trodden under foot, and the bloody (if it couldn't be done otherwise) repression of tyrants. That is what we were chiefly interested in at the time.

My aunt* didn't like the printing press. She was tall and narrow-shouldered and stooping. She had a broad, high nose, and a long, rather severe face. She kept her mouth shut tight except when she was speaking, and her lips jutted out a little, especially when she was thinking about something interesting.

She was always moving about very quickly over the house. She used to sweep into the schoolroom early in the morning in a brown cloth dressing-gown, when we were having lessons, and listen for a minute. Then she would whirl the governess out of her chair and give us the lessons herself. She knew how to hit on the parts we knew least. Her voice went very high and very low, and she explained beautifully. Whenever my uncle gave me half-a-crown to spend she took it away to buy my stockings with. She loved me, but she thought that children should be taught to be economical. She was very clever and used to lecture about the rights of women; and she had written several books and painted pictures. She knew a great deal about education. Sometimes she whipped her children when they fell down and hurt

*Mrs. Rossetti was the eldest daughter of Ford Madox-Brown.

themselves, to teach them to be more careful, but she never did at any other time. In the afternoon when she was not busy she would nearly always smile and answer the most difficult questions.

She used to sweep along the streets just as quickly as she swept about the house. When we went out with her we used to follow in a tail quite out of breath.

She said that no one had the right to spend one idle moment on this globe. If she couldn't write or teach and lecture she would scrub, or sweep the streets, or clean drains rather than be idle. She said work, work, work, was the object of life.

She wore quite old clothes in the street, because she said it was wrong to spend much money on clothes. She cut down Olive's dresses for Helen when Olive had done with them, and cut them still smaller for Mary when Helen had. She ate up all the fat and gristly pieces on her plate because she said luxurious habits were detestable and she made us eat them too, except Helen, because she was delicate.

She was very kind to the poor. Once we met a man in Tottenham Court Road, and he asked her for a penny to buy some food. She went into a shop and bought a big white roll for him and a hunk of cheese. When she came out and gave it to him, he opened it and said, quite quietly and not angrily at all, "You might have stood a pat of butter, Madam," and she looked at him and went back into the shop and paid the shopman to cut the roll and spread some butter on it. Then the man began to eat it at once. We thought she would have been angry, but she was not, only thoughtful.

Sometimes she would say, "And now we'll go and see Christina,"* and we did so.

She was a very kind poetess who lived in one of a row of houses in Torrington Square and wrote poems that usually ended sadly. She was very religious, and sometimes she used to put on a long black veil and go into a sisterhood to pray. But at other times she wore a black dress and a white lace cap, and we used to find her in the back room of her house with her hands folded, thinking and waiting for the kettle to boil. But, of course, she did other things as well. Once she made me a tiny dining-room table and half a dozen chairs out of chestnuts and pins and red string, and put them in a little box and gave them to me and said, "When you look at them, remember Aunt Christina," and I did.

She had a mild religious face, and smooth hair, and very big grey eyes, rather prominent. When we came in she was always glad, and she used to say, "Welcome, merry little maidens," and made us sit round the table and have tea, and eat as much as we wanted. She had a big cupboard with sweets in it, and a glass tank full of gold-fish, and two very ancient ugly aunts who lay in

*Christina Rossetti.

7

beds on the opposite sides of a room, with a strip of carpet in the middle.

They were so old that they couldn't stand up, and they could hardly talk. They always seemed to me to be waving their long skinny hands. They wore big nightcaps with frills round the edges and flowered bed-jackets.

They were very fond of children and, after tea, I used to be sent up for them to look at. They used to stretch out their hands to me, and I used to stand on the strip of carpet between them and seem rude and unwilling to make friends. But it was really because I was frightened, for they reminded me of the wolf when he had eaten Red-Riding-Hood's grandmother up, and put on her nightcap and got into bed. They were, in fact, very affectionate, and wanted to be kind to me. It was only because they were so old and dried and wrinkled that I was frightened.

The reason that my aunt disliked the printing machine was that the day on which the paper went to press we were all quite black with the part that comes off on your hands and face, and Olive and Arthur were hot and irritable. Besides, she said, it was not right for my uncle, who was employed by the Government, to have a paper of that kind printed in his house. When people of importance came to see my uncle it could be heard quite plainly from his study, groaning in the basement. But Uncle William stood up for us and protected it.

He had a head and face that, joined together, were an exact oval. His head was perfectly bald and shiny on the top, but he had a little white tufty fringe at the back that reached right down to his collar. He was tall and rather bent, and he wore a black frock-coat with a turn-down collar, and rather wide trousers. He had thick white eyebrows and dark eyes. We loved him almost better than any one, because he was so gentle and stuck to us through thick and thin about everything, not only about the printing press. He always read the articles in the paper, and he would smile and make suggestions in his kind soft voice. But he always said to us, "Don't you think so?" not at all as if he really knew better than we. Aunt Lucy didn't really keep the page-boy so much for his mother's sake as that Uncle William protected him and said he had an interesting character, and he was going to send him to the Polytechnic.

❧❧❧

We three little ones had a special mission of our own, although it was all part of the same work. It was the reformation of policemen. Of course, we understood very well that if we could get them on our side it would be a very great thing. We felt nervous when we undertook the work, but Olive told us that that kind of agitation was quite within the law until the policemen had actually *begun* to rebel against their chiefs. Then, of course, it would be a case of save yourself whoever can. I think she looked it up in some sort of Blue Book before we started. She was always getting worried and looking things up because she was so anxious that no mistakes should be made.

What we had to explain to the police was that it was most unfair to put a man in prison merely for taking what he needed from another man who had more than the first man had. There are so many riches in the world that there is no reason why every man should not have enough for himself, and if the second man has too much and can't be persuaded by kindness to share it with the first man who hasn't enough, then the first man has every right to take it from the second by force. The second man depends entirely upon the armed supporters of the law, who are the police and military, to aid and abet him in his greediness, and every right-minded policeman should feel ashamed to strike a blow in such a horrid cause. That was our programme in a nutshell.

We took our banner, the smaller one, with us to give us confidence, and we arranged it as we went along. We had simply to hem the police in as they stood at their corners, so that we could force them to listen to us. I was to stand in the middle holding the banner in front of me, and I was to begin the address.

The policeman nearest to us was at the corner of Avenue Road in the St. John's Wood Road. We came down from Primrose Hill in a row, with the banner flying. We didn't mind the people stopping to stare after us. We were used to being stared at, even when we hadn't got the banner with us, because Aunt Lucy always dressed us in artistic style, and we were busy listening to Helen explaining to us exactly what to do. We took some copies of the paper with us, but the police were not to pay for them.

Helen really thought that there might be some chance of our being arrested and dragged off to prison, but she said we were not to mind because other people had been through far worse. She said that the police did really sometimes go beyond their duty, but that we were in the right, and we ought to be ready to die if necessary. But in any case, there was not the slightest danger of our being executed or anything really serious. She herself wouldn't have minded being executed in the very least. She didn't say so, but I'm sure she wouldn't. She was very brave, although she had a cough, and was so thin and delicate. Once she cut her finger open and wrote a document in her own blood, swearing that when she was dead she would rise from the grave if it were possible and walk into our bedroom so that we might really know once for all whether it were possible for the spirit to exist without the body or not. Helen thought she was going to die quite soon because of her weak chest, and other people thought so too. But she wasn't at all frightened. She said it was absolutely the only way of finding out for certain several things she wanted to know. She was not religious. Once she put Mary's doll out on the bedroom window-sill in the soaking rain, and made us pray to God to keep it dry as a sign that He really did exist and was able to do anything He wanted. When we took it in the morning, you wouldn't have known it for the same creature. Helen said that it was a sure sign that there wasn't any God, because if there had been He would have been only too happy to have saved our souls by anything so simple. Mary nearly cried when she saw the *sodden shapeless mass*. But she stopped herself because she had really meant to offer it as a sacrifice. She thought it meant that there *was* a God and He had wanted to punish us for being so presumptuous and uncertain. Helen did not have dolls, or she would have used one of her own. We buried her document behind a loose brick in the old wall at the bottom of Acacia Road, and whenever we went past she made a sort of Freemason sign with her finger to show that she remembered it and was going to keep her vow.

Mary was so frightened by what Helen had said about the executions that she had nearly begun to cry before we reached the bottom of St. Edmund's Terrace, which was quite near the first policeman. She was afraid we really might be executed by some mistake. She said that terrible mistakes were made. Once a poor man was hanged three times and nearly killed before they found out it wasn't the right man. If the rope hadn't broken they'd never have found out then.

I felt sorry for Mary. She was small and fat and her face was broad. She often used to get anxious about things. She liked digging up remains in the back garden and wondering what they were. Once she dug up some bones and was certain they belonged to a victim who had been buried by a murderer, as you read about it in the paper. She was very frightened, but Helen said no, they were some chicken bones abandoned by the cat; and so they were. And she dug up a scrap of paper, and was sure she could see traces of a mysterious message written on it, but we couldn't see anything. We put it under the microscope, and there was nothing written on it at all. But she said she could see it, so she kept it. When she dug up an old piece of glass or tin she used to believe they were Roman remains, because she said she was sure it was the Romans who had begun to build the waterworks at the foot of Primrose Hill. She didn't believe it really, but she wanted to so much that she almost did. She wasn't very brave, and she used to cry a good deal because she was always being frightened by the grave things Helen talked about.

Helen stopped short in the middle of the road and began to scold her. Her face was quite white with anger. She said, "Coward, coward, coward, only fit for nursing dolls and hemming pocket handkerchiefs." She said we must fight, fight, fight. All the great men and women in the world had lived fighting and died fighting. If we were afraid of a perfectly peaceful policeman now where should we be when the social revolution came?

She began to cough in the middle, and Mary gave way at once. Every one gave way to her when she began to cough, because it made them so sorry for her. It shook her so and made her look so thin and ill.

I secretly hoped that the policeman would not be at his corner. But he was. He had just settled down in it again after a short walk to and fro. He wasn't going to move again just then.

He was a very broad and tall policeman with a large head and fat red cheeks. His eyes were blue and turned up at the corners. They weren't bright, but they were very gay and kind.

We stood in a row in front of him just as we had said we would. I held the banner with one hand and the papers with the other, so I felt that I was rooted to the spot. It was a horrid feeling.

I fancy he must have thought us very small, because he stooped right down with a hand on each knee to look at us. He smiled right across his face. He was just like the giant in our picture book when he stooped down and looked at Jack and was thinking how glad he was that he was going to eat him.

His face was quite near mine, and I felt sure that he was going to take a bite out of my cheek. But it was the banner that attracted him. He was trying to read what was pasted on it, but I knew he couldn't because some of the letters were turned the wrong way round, and they were a good many different sizes.

He said, "That's a pretty thing you've got there; what's writ across it?"

His voice was a little hoarse as though he used to have a sore throat rather often. I daresay it was ruined by standing in the damp. But he himself was not rough.

I knew what I ought to say, but I couldn't think of it. It was because of the banner and the papers, and being rather near. If I could have run across the road and stood on the other side I could have explained quite well.

I held up the literature and said, "Would you read the paper, please?"

This was stupid, because of course he wouldn't want to read the paper until he had had it properly explained to him.

Mary's eyes and mouth were quite wide open, she was so frightened. Helen couldn't wait any longer. She was always impatient. She began to help and she did it beautifully.

First, she pointed out each word on the banner with her finger and explained exactly what it meant, and the policeman was interested. Then she flung the hair back off her shoulder and put her hand on her hip. She always stood like that when she was giving explanations. Her face looked very affectionate and truthful, and her voice went up and down a little, something like Aunt Lucy's. She explained our whole programme from beginning to end, not only that part especially for the use of the police.

She said there was no reason why policemen shouldn't have things just as nice as a king. They were both human beings. It was only just an *accident* that one had been born a king and the other a policeman. If the other had been born a king and the one a policeman nobody would ever have noticed the difference. A policeman was as good as any king, in fact, better, because he was honest and cheap and worked for his living, while a king was useless and expensive, and only kept for showing off.

The policeman hitched up his belt with both his thumbs and said, "Ah, that's what they call Socialism, that is. What's yours is mine, and what's mine's my own sort o' business, eh?"

Helen said, "What is is everybody's," very gravely.

"That'll want a deal o' putting straight, that will, if ever that comes in," said the policeman, and he hitched himself up all round again and stamped both his feet, first one and then the other. "That'll take a deal o' thinking of."

"Well, but will you think about it?" Helen said. Her face looked shining and transparent like the face of the little boy Christ talking to the old Jews in the picture in the Tate Gallery.

"Ah, but it wants wiser heads than mine to think about it," said the policeman. "All the thinking I could do wouldn't make it come no clearer. You want a lot of learning to understand such things. People says one thing, and people says another, and from what I can hear they're all a-contradicting of 'emselves and of each other. I don't take much notice of it."

"Well, but will you read the paper?" Helen said. "You'll find a lot about it there. I am sure it will be a help to you."

"*Will* I read the paper?" he said, "of course I will." And I gave him one and he took it in his great podgy hand and wrenched himself round and hoisted up his coat tails and rammed it down into his trousers pocket. Then he swung himself straight again, and bobbed up and down and jerked his knees in and out, and stooped again and touched my face with his first finger. It felt just as big and heavy as one of those long leathery sausages we used to have for supper before the page-boy's mother came.

17

"I never seen cheeks so red, nor yet eyes so blue," he said, "and what a lot of hair, as soft as silk. I reckon you don't like havin' that brushed out of a evenin'!"

I didn't know what to say. One never does when people make personal remarks.

"I got a little lass your size," he said, "with hair that colour, and she makes a rare fuss when her mother puts it into papers of a evenin'."

❦❦❦

Mary crept into my bed in the night. We had three beds in a row in the night nursery. She was quite cold and frightened again. She couldn't forget the poor man who had been hanged three times. But she said, "Don't tell Helen because she'll say 'coward, coward, coward,' and I can't bear it."

She simply worshipped Helen. She used to stand sometimes for a long time quite still behind her chair in the schoolroom when she was doing her lessons in the evening. Sometimes she would stroke her hair quite gently, and Helen would fling it back off her shoulder and flash round and say, "Oh, bother you!" and Mary used to say, "I didn't think you'd feel it," and stand still again. When Helen wrote the bloody document about beyond the grave Mary cried because she couldn't bear to think that Helen might be going to die. Only she always said, "Don't tell Helen," because Helen would have *scorned* her for it.

18

I tried to comfort her about the man who had been hanged three times. I said I'd make a poem about it, and she wouldn't be frightened any more when she saw it properly explained. The first verse came at once as soon as I began to think about it,

> *Three times, three times was he strung up,*
> *Three times, three times he fell,*
> *The minions of the law were there,*
> *The clergyman as well . . .*

I wrote poems about everything that interested me. I had a whole book full of them. Some were very sad, and some were cheerful. One began,

> *A bloody, bloody King thou wast!*

It was called "An Ode to King John," but Helen looked over my shoulder and put in "Or any King," in brackets. She was a dreadful enemy of kings. I wrote the ode after Aunt Lucy read us about how King John had tried to put out Prince Arthur's eyes in Shakespeare's play.

When I thought of a new poem in the night I used to escape from the governess early in the morning and run down to my aunt's bedroom to tell her about it. I sat on a chair beside the dressing-table while she was twisting her hair up, in her petticoat-bodice in front of the glass. I recited the poem before it was written down.

Uncle William would be in bed with his nice white

nightcap on and the sheets up to his chin. He used to raise himself up on his elbow to listen, and he used to laugh and say, "Bravo, bravo, my little girl!"

And Aunt Lucy used to leave go of her hair and stoop down and kiss me and tell me what she thought about it. She always said at the end, "Write about everything that interests you, little dear, and if you can't write it in poetry, write it in prose."

And I did. I wrote a book of stories besides, and a play in verse. But it hadn't enough *incident* in it to be acted.

❧❧❧

On Sundays we used to go to make propaganda in Hyde Park. Olive and Arthur took charge of the big banner, and we distributed the little banner and the literature among ourselves. We used to go by train and fold the banners up and put them in the luggage rack when we got in, and we sold the paper on the platform till the train came in.

Olive wore a round black astrakhan cap, and a short black coat with astrakhan on the collar and sleeves, and a green skirt. She and Arthur both had auburn hair. Olive's nose was short and her face was very serious and covered with freckles. So was Arthur's, but they were more difficult to see on his, because it nearly always was rather dirty.

Olive was of a worrying nature. She was always wondering whether we had mislaid one of the banners, or

20

whether we hadn't given too much change when we were paid for the literature, or whether we weren't letting wrong ideas creep into the programme. She had quite a pucker in her forehead through always worrying so much. She said it made it worse because Arthur was no help to her in practical things. It wasn't that he wasn't keen, but he was so absent-minded. He used to forget all sorts of things. He very often forgot to wash himself and do his hair in the morning, and it wasn't that he didn't want to, because he didn't mind in the least when other people washed him. As a rule, when he was sent up to get clean before meals he did not come down again until he was fetched, and then he was still quite cloudy. If anybody wanted to take him out to lunch or tea, the only thing for them to do was to wash him themselves very carefully and keep tight hold of him till they started.

He used to wander off in the most excruciating moments, just when the paper was going to press, and go into the day-nursery and make noisy experiments. He liked to fill a tin with gas and close it and hold it over a flame until the lid flew off with a tremendous bang, and once he blew his hair and eyebrows off by an experiment with gunpowder, which nobody ever knew how he got. Once we found him standing on the balcony with an experimented-upon umbrella in his hand. He said that when he jumped it would open and he would descend into the garden, like a parachutist from a balloon. But, if it hadn't opened, he would certainly have been killed. Olive was waiting in agonies in the printing room for him to finish off his leading article, because, although he was so unreliable, she didn't feel it was safe to do anything like that without him.

He had a deep cracked voice, and a big forehead like his uncle's, the celebrated poet and painter, and round brown eyes that sometimes looked as bright as though they had a red light lit behind them. Sometimes he would stare in such a wild and interested way that you couldn't help looking round to see if anything was there, though you knew there could be nothing.

Once Olive stationed him at Baker Street Station with a pile of the literature to sell, and when she came back in an hour to see how he was getting on she found him striding up and down the platform and talking to himself with the literature all hanging floppily over his arm. Of course, he hadn't sold a single copy. We used to meet him charging down from the top of Primrose Hill in his black ulster, with his hat over his eyes, brandishing a book, talking to himself, and waving his arms about like a madman. He was always reading. He read at meals, in the street, and in bed, and in his bath. He read very serious books, and Uncle William gave him a special key to the bookcase in the library where all his most precious ones were kept. He trusted him entirely, because they were the only things he never lost. His articles were the best in the paper. Once an important social reformer* came to the house. He wore a blue serge suit, and he had a great deal of fluffy grey hair standing up all round his head, and a frizzy beard, rather a flushed face, and a beautifully shaped nose. He stood upon the hearthrug and we all sat round and gazed at him in adoration. Arthur was especially introduced to him and he said, "I congratulate you, young sir, on a particularly clever piece of writing."

It was Arthur's article in the last number, and he asked if he would like to come and give a paper on the subject in his club at Hammersmith. Arthur would have agreed, but Aunt Lucy said "No," that he had still a great deal to learn himself before he could begin to think of teaching other people.

He and Olive wrote a play in the correct Greek style, with a Chorus in white robes, waving long grass. It was acted in the drawing-room, and a great many people came to see it. We were the Chorus, and told the people exactly what was going on. Aunt Lucy made the robes out of butter muslin. She was the prompter and sat in the wings, but we really didn't want much prompting for Olive had rehearsed us all so carefully.

Arthur was a youth who slew a loathsome monster. Aunt Lucy pulled it in on a thread from the other wings

*William Morris.

for him to rush upon. He stood in the middle of the stage with his foot upon its neck and slew it so fiercely that all the people were astonished and said that he would make a splendid actor. But it wasn't really acting. He simply was so absent-minded that he imagined that he really was the youth. He was in butter muslin too, but it was tied in round the waist. We made his sword out of cardboard and covered it with gold paper. He had on sandals laced with gold paper half-way up his legs, and a gold band in his hair. He had to let his hair grow long for some time beforehand, but he was glad because he hated going to the barber's. Olive was worried for fear he should split the laces of his sandals in his emotion, but luckily he didn't. The people in front said he scowled so savagely that his face looked quite terrible, and the perspiration poured off him with excitement. I quite believed it, for I knew how worked up he used to be when we met him in his ulster on Primrose Hill.

Our banners were not so noticeable in the Park, because there were so many others there. There were some speakers called Iconoclasts, and some called Socialists, and some called Humanitarians, and some called Unitarians, and some called Vegetarians; and they stood, each under their own banner, giving explanations. Some of the crowd stood and listened and groaned and clapped and hissed and asked questions and made rude remarks, and some just walked about and took no notice. We planted our banner down near the Socialists as a meeting-place, and mixed with the crowd to sell literature and gather information. Olive told us if ever we met with anything of interest to jot it down with pencil in our note-books, and we did. If any one said anything very wise or noble we handed him a pencil and asked him for his autograph. I called out "*The Torch*," "*The Torch*," to attract the people to the literature, and some mocking boys said it was like a mouse squeaking in the larder. People turned round and said, "What a funny little girl!" and "Bless her, what has she got there?" and they bought the paper just to see. Olive explained hard all the time she sold the literature. She wasn't upset at all even when quite a crowd came round her. She frowned and explained all the harder. They tried to get her in a corner, asking unfriendly questions, but she was too clever for them, and besides, she had looked it all up beforehand, while they hadn't, and she had a lot of practice on us too. Arthur generally got lost at once and turned up when the Park was nearly empty, talking to somebody he didn't know. But he was not at all confused.

We had a cigar box full of autographs of the speakers in the Park, and we used to rummage our fingers in them when we wanted inspiration. Once there was a very desperate and famous lady* there, and people said we should never be able to get her autograph, because she

*Louise Michel.

always refused to give it. But we thought we'd try. Olive went up to ask her first in case she wanted explanations, but a tall stooping gentleman in a foreign hat, with his hands behind his back and hair that flowed and mingled with his beard, whom she was talking to, stepped in front of her and said that "Madame" could not be disturbed.

We gathered round the banner and considered what to do. Helen said that I ought to be sent because nobody was likely to take me for a spy. I went up to the lady and pulled her sleeve, and the foreign gentleman jumped forward again, and I was frightened. But she had turned round and seen me first, and she sat down in a chair behind her and pulled me up against her and asked me what I wanted. I told her, and she laughed and said, "What a rosy little girl!"

She was very thin, and she was dressed all in black. Her face had dry grey skin on it, and her hair was grey, and I thought she must be grey all over, underneath her clothes as well. She had thin lips and a long pointed nose and little eyes. They were very bright and sharp, but not very kind. I said please was it really true that she had been in prison? I thought that as she was a lady there might be some mistake. She said it was quite true, and what had little girls to do with things like that? I said I was connected with a paper, and did she mind, and was she much afraid (when she was put in prison)? Her face

26

looked very brave, and she said she was never afraid, and that she minded nothing, because she knew that all the while the world was getting better, and that people would be cleverer and happier. She stroked my cheek and smiled again and asked me, did I understand? And I said, "Oh, yes, that's what we think too"—after the Social Revolution. She asked me what my name was, and I said, "Poppy," and the foreign gentleman translated it into French, and she laughed again and said, "That is quite right; thus it must be." I said, would she please be so kind as to give me her autograph, because my cousins wanted it badly. And she said, "Where are your cousins?" and we looked round and we couldn't see them because they were out of sight behind the banner. They had promised not to peep, or I should have been too shy to ask her. She took my pencil and wrote L——— M——— right across the paper in long thick crooked letters. And I thanked her very much and said good-bye, and she took my face between her hands and looked at it and smiled and said, "Good-bye, nice little girl." And she looked after me till I had got right back to the banner, and then I looked round and she waved her hand to me and smiled again.

❖

CHAPTER TWO

In My Grandfather's House

My grandfather lived in the house next door but one to us. He was the celebrated painter, F. M. B.* He was one of the kindest, gentlest, handsomest old gentlemen that ever lived. Everybody loved him. He wore a blue cloth tam-o'-shanter when he was at work, and in the winter sat with his legs in a big bag made of fur inside, like those worn at the North Pole. His cheeks were pink, and he had blue eyes, and his hair fell straight down on both sides of his face nearly to the bottom of his ears, and my grandmother cut it straight and even all the way round behind. It was wonderfully thick and pure snow white, and so was his beard. He wasn't very tall, but his shoulders were broad, and he looked somehow grand and im-

*Ford Madox-Brown.

portant. He nearly always smiled when you looked at him, not an empty smile, but a kind, understanding one, though his eyes looked quite sad all the while. His lips jutted out when he was thoughtful, something like Aunt Lucy's, and then they looked terribly stern. He usually wore a shiny top-hat and a black cape, and he used to take my grandmother's little dog out for a walk on Primrose Hill. He couldn't walk very fast, because he had the gout, but the little dog was very old and couldn't go fast either, so it didn't mind. He would stop from time to time and look behind to see if it was coming, and then it used to stop too, and sit down and look up at him and hang its tongue out and wag its tail, and they went on again.

Sometimes he smiled a different sort of smile—his whole face looked as if it were laughing and his eyes as well. But that was very rarely. Once, when he was having breakfast with a good many people one of his letters said that two very important people were coming to see his last big picture before it left the house. He looked round the table and said, "That will mean quite an expenditure on red carpet."

And then he smiled the second sort of smile. You felt just as if the sun had come out and begun to shine and made everything warm all of a sudden when you didn't expect it. Nobody could help laughing. I didn't know why he was so amused, but I knew he was, because he never smiled like that unless he had heard something really funny.

When I told Helen she was very much upset. She kept popping up and down all through morning preparation time and couldn't do her lessons. At last she grabbed her tape-measure and ran out of the schoolroom and down the stairs into the hall, and she measured the whole distance right from the bottom of the stairs through the hall and down the front steps to the edge of the pavement to see how much red carpet would be needed. She was very angry. She said it would mean thirteen yards at least, and it must be five shillings a yard for a good quality. She couldn't bear to think that the important persons were going to have so much money spent upon them. But they got ill and didn't come after all, and it was a good thing they didn't, or they might have had a dreadful surprise prepared for them in the house next door but one.

My grandfather told stories so well that some people said he did it better than anybody else in London, and you never got tired of them because they were a little different each time. When he told them in the studio he would walk up and down and wave his brush or painting-stick, and once at dinner he began to wave the carving-knife because he suddenly thought of a story just when he was carving the joint. There was an artist there, who was so hungry that he couldn't stand it any longer. So he made up a little verse and recited it aloud:

> *When B. carves*
> *Everybody starves.*

Then my grandfather remembered and gave him some meat.

Sometimes he used to be very angry, thought not seriously. When the cook sent up some nice pudding at dinner which he couldn't eat because of his gout he used to fly into a passion and bang his fists on the table and say, "Damn that woman, why does she always go on cooking things I mustn't eat?"

But the next minute he'd forget about it and smile at us all round the table as much as to say, "Aren't I silly to make such a fuss about a pudding?" and as if he hoped we might all enjoy the pudding, although he couldn't eat it. He used to be angry too when he pushed his spectacles up on the top of his head and lost them. He would look for them all over the studio, and rummage for them on his great big table, and thump upon it angrily, because he said the housemaid must have moved them when she dusted it. But when I said, "Why, grandpapa, they're up on top of your head all the time," he used to smile at once and fetch them down and say, "Why, bless me, little pigeon, so they are."

Once a gentleman came to the house to bring my mother some money from the Queen, because my father had died too young for her to have a pension and she was very poor. When my grandfather was told about it he flew into a frightful rage. We heard him quite plainly shouting in the studio, "Where are my boots?"

And he put his boots on and stumped down to the drawing-room where the gentleman was waiting, who was very much alarmed. And when my grandfather saw how nervous he was he was sorry for him. He refused to take the money, but opened the door for him quite politely, and said as he went out, "Tell Her Majesty my daughter is not a beggar."

My grandfather always bought our paper—*The Torch*—and he agreed with us in almost everything. He hated tyrants and proud rich people. When we told him of something that tyrants had been doing he used to frown and look extremely fierce and say, "God bless us, the abominable villains!"

He asked us to tell him about everything, and we always did. He loved us all exceedingly, but he was kindest of all to me, because my father hadn't very long been dead. When I ran in to see him in the morning he used to say to me, "Little pigeon, little pigeon, you're looking very paintable to-day," and would let me sit by him in the studio when he was working.

He had a very large studio with a lot of pictures on

easels in it, and a weak lay-figure with false yellow hair that was nearly always propped up behind the door. It had stupid round glass eyes that were always staring, and no expression at all in its face. It never stood quite straight because its joints were loose. The slightest jolt used to make it jump all over and stand in quite a different position. You looked at it one moment and its head was straight and it was looking in front of it with its arms folded as if it had settled down like that for the day, and when you turned round again it would be staring over its shoulder out of the window with one arm straight down and the other sticking out to one side. That was because a cart had gone past or some one had moved about in the room overhead.

At night I used to fly past the studio, because I knew it was there behind the door ready to move in a moment, and when I was in the studio I used to turn round every minute to see what it was doing. I would not have kept it had I been my grandfather, but he did because it reminded him of one of his friends.

He used to paint on top of a kind of square barrel. It had a big thick screw coming up out of the middle of it, and on the top of the screw there was a chair, and when you turned it round it went up and up till it seemed to be going right through the ceiling. My grandfather used to put his tam-o'-shanter on and climb on to the barrel off a small step-ladder and ask somebody to wind him up on the chair. That was when he was painting a very big and high picture. It stretched right across the longest wall of the studio and reached nearly to the ceiling. There was a regiment of soldiers in the picture, and a barge on a canal with a beautiful dark woman sitting in it, nursing twins. They were really only one baby, but when my grandfather had finished painting it in one arm the woman turned it over and held it in the other, and then he painted it as a twin.

He would rather have had real twins, but the proper kind of baby was so difficult to find. He was very particular. First all the babies came in from the mews at the corner for him to look at. He was kind to them, but they did not please him because they weren't good looking, and their mothers were hurt and took them back again. We used to stop in the street and look at the nicely dressed babies in perambulators, but they were too refined. Then we went to a baby show in Camden Town, where a lot of women were sitting round the room on chairs with babies. Some were screaming and throwing themselves about, but some just looked on and took no notice. One lady in spectacles was weighing babies in scales, and the other was writing about them in a book. She was very pleased to see us, and she said, "Any of the mothers would be honoured and delighted." We went round looking at the babies, and the mothers were anxious and began to put their caps on straight and smooth their bibs and pull their dresses up to show how fat their legs were. But they weren't really very fat, because they were quite poor babies. But at last we found a very fat and red one sitting in a corner. It was fatter than any of the others, because a well-known lady writer had been kind to it and sent her milkman to its mother every day, so that it could have as much milk as it wanted. My grandfather said, "That's a remarkable baby," and it opened its eyes and mouth and stared, and the mother screwed up her face and was pleased and said, "I'm sure you're very kind," and jumped the baby up and down. And all the other mothers stared with their mouths open, but the babies themselves were not at all interested.

The fat baby came next day in a mail-cart, and it was so fashionably dressed in white that it pricked you wherever you touched it because of the starch. It didn't cry when its mother left it in the studio, and she said that was the best of cow's milk from the first. When she had gone we took off its fashionable clothes and put them away in the cupboard very carefully, and we dressed it in a soft little petticoat with short sleeves and a little round cap that my mother used to wear when she was a baby. It turned its head round and opened its mouth and stared hard all the time, and seemed very much surprised, but it didn't mind. It was delightfully soft and slippery. There was a little girl in the picture too, with long golden hair, stretching up on tiptoe with her arms up begging her mother for a sip out of her glass of wine. I was the little girl, and when I got tired of stretching my arms up for the wine I had them held up on both sides of me, like Moses on the mountain when he was too tired to go on praying any longer.

I used to sit on a footstool beside my grandfather's chair. He was very high and I was very low, and I used to draw faces on a piece of paper. But I had no talent. When the face seemed to me too ugly that I couldn't stand it any longer I used to look up and say, "Grand-papa, it isn't coming nicely."

And he would look down from his chair and say, "Isn't it? Let me see what's wrong with it."

And he used to wind himself down and take off his cap and push his spectacles on to the top of his head, while I stood on tiptoe and handed up the paper for him to make corrections. He used to say, "Ah, you see, the nose turns up too sharply at the end," or "Lips don't twist up so tightly into one another as you've made them here," and he'd take the pencil and put it all straight in a moment, and make it quite a handsome, interesting face. I said, "Thank you, grandpapa, and don't forget that your spectacles are on top of your head again."

All sorts of odd people used to come to the studio. Some were models and some were just visitors. The models were generally very proud of some part of their bodies. Some praised their shoulders, and some praised their feet. One lady said she had one of the most beautiful backs the sun had ever shone upon. She was most obstinate about it and didn't wish to go away. She said my grandfather couldn't help being delighted with her back if only she were allowed to take her clothes off. But she was not allowed to. Once an ambassador came to tea with a little dog under his arm, and said it would only drink milk with cream in it out of a china saucer. It was quite true, so that we had to send round to the dairy for some cream because there wasn't any in the house, and when Aunt Lucy heard of it she said that it was criminal extravagance. One extremely dirty old man with very long hair and a white beard arrived in a hansom cab. He said that once he had washed and been painted as King Lear, but it didn't really pay him, because beggars were much more popular. As a matter of fact, he was not so very poor, but he kept himself dirty on purpose, in order to look like a beggar. He said, if the worst came to the worst he could always earn something as a blind man led by a boy outside the pits of theatres, though he was not blind at all.

Once a poetess came to be painted by a long, nervous artist who was a pupil of my grandfather's. He wore very big spectacles because he was short-sighted, and he had a curious squeaky voice. His beard was not like an ordinary beard, but looked like separate tufts of hair pasted

37

on all over his chin and beneath his nose. He was very excitable. Once when my grandfather was unable to get a suitable model for Sardanapolus, the artist dragged a barrel organ all the way home from St. John's Wood Station with the Italian organ-grinder running behind him and scolding indignantly, because he thought he would look so splendid as Sardanapolus lying on the sofa. The organ-grinder really was the right type, but he refused. He said that nothing should induce him to take off his clothes in such a climate, and that without music no Southerner could stand it. So he went away and wouldn't come again. My grandfather said he was sure it was because the man was frightened and thought we were all mad.

The poetess* had curly black hair and a hooked nose, and rather a brown face. She put on a black velvet dress to be painted in, and held a big bunch of poppies in her hand. She quarrelled with the artist, and they made a great noise. She said he made her face look like a piece of gingerbread, and that the poppies were like dabs of scarlet flannel, and he said he had never been spoken to like that in his life before. They talked so loudly, and were so rude to one another, that my grandfather began to climb down from his painting chair to see what it was all about. And just when he had got up to the picture and was going to look at it the artist put his face down on his

*Mathilde Blind.

shoulder and burst into tears. Grandpapa said, "Be a man now, H., and control yourself," and was most kind and patient and tried to make them friends. But the poetess would not be reconciled. She cast a furious look at him and swept out of the room and collided with Aunt Lucy, who was coming up the stairs. Sometimes a crowd of fashionable people came all together to look at the pictures, and then my grandfather changed his coat, and that was called a "Private View."

❦❦❦

I can't remember my grandmother's* face as plainly as most people's, though she had only been dead a short time then. She was very, very kind and gentle, and when she took me in her arms they were soft, and a sweet scent came from her shawl; not like scent bought at shops, but like that of herbs and flowers growing in the country. She was so gentle that whenever she came into a room where people were quarrelling they stopped and behaved properly. It was said that when she was a baby lying in her cradle the ghost of a huntsman came into the room and picked her up and looked at her sadly and sighed and put her down again. She wasn't old and bent at all, but tall and straight, and her voice was so soft that sometimes you'd hardly know that she was speaking. She used to move about the house a great deal like Aunt Lucy, but more slowly, and her skirts made a pretty

*Mrs. Ford Madox-Brown.

39

sound when she moved. She often carried a little basket and a big bunch of keys in her hands. She used to go right down the stairs to the big storeroom next the kitchen, and I went in after her and sat down on a stool and watched her, and she would give me a stick of chocolate. When she moved from one shelf to another her dress made the nice sighing sound and smelt countrified even among all the cookery things. She was always taking care of my grandfather and trying to make people pleased and give them what they wanted. Once when she was young, and it was a very cold winter, and many men were out of work and their little children hungry, she turned her drawing-room into a soup-kitchen and made soup for them and fed them. She was quite poor then, and had to go without all sorts of things herself to get the money. Nothing ever made her angry. When my grandfather flew into a rage she used to smile and say, "Ford, Ford," and he was quiet at once, and began smiling.

When she was ill she was sorry for giving people trouble and for making them run up and down the stairs. She used to say to me, "Thank you, little grand-daughter, and you must forgive me, for, you see, I'm ill. I shan't be able to get up any more and go down to the storeroom with you as I used to do."

She used to make me sprinkle breadcrumbs on her window-sill for the little robin that came and looked in at her window every morning, and she said, "One day he'll come and look in like that, and I shan't be here."

Once in the night, just before she died, when she'd forgotten all about the world already, she began to sing a song, but very gently, and my grandfather said her voice was just as sweet as when she was a girl and they used to sing it together.

He was terribly unhappy when she died. He used to sit alone in the studio for hours together, doing no work at all. Once when I went in to him he turned round and looked at me with an odd far-away expression as if he didn't see me. I was surprised, and I ran to him and said, "Grandpapa, have you lost something?"

And he looked at me and smiled and said, "Oh, it's little pigeon. Yes, my little pigeon, yes, I have." He took me in between his knees and held me, and I climbed on to his lap and put my head on his shoulder, and we didn't move again till it was nearly dark.

In the evening he used to wander up and down and in and out from room to room, as if he were looking everywhere to try and find my grandmother. One night I heard him coming down the stairs, and I was frightened because it was night and because I knew his face would look so sad and strange. I slipped into the dining-room and sat down behind the door. He came in and looked all round the room, but it was nearly dark and he didn't see me. Then he went out and into the drawing-room to look there too, then out again and up the stairs. I slipped off my chair and crept out into the hall to look, and when he was half-way up the stairs he stopped and leant his head down on the bannisters and his shoulders moved up and down and he was sobbing. I went into the drawing-room because I thought there might be some one there. But there was nobody, and I went out into the hall again. The big clock in the hall was going tick, tick, as it always did, and the gas was turned low, and the beautiful gold paper on the wall looked dim. It was very still and lonely, and there were big shadows everywhere. A long way away down the stairs I could hear the servants laughing and having supper in the kitchen, but there was no other sound. My grandfather went on slowly up the stairs, and I went back into the drawing-room and lay down on the sofa in the dark and began to cry because I wanted to see my father and I couldn't, and because my grandfather was so unhappy, and because of all the kind dead people who used to be so loving and protecting. But, however much you want them and however much you cry, they'll never hear you, and they'll never come back again.

❧❧❧

The kitchen was at the end of a stone passage at the foot of a flight of stone steps. I liked to go there, but I was not really allowed to. I liked it best of all in the evening when the servants had finished supper, and sometimes the cook would let me sit on a chair in the corner near the stove. She was rather an ill-tempered cook, though she often used to laugh. She had been in the family ever since my mother was quite a little girl. She had a dark yellow face and brown eyes and black hair. It was quite straight like tape, and she scraped it back from her forehead and did it in a funny knob behind. It wasn't black really, but she used an excellent hair dye, and said, what did it matter if it came off on the pillow-cases? She said nobody need look their age if only they would take the trouble to look young. But she didn't look young herself, because she was so bony and her face so dreadfully wrinkled. She looked very nice though when she laughed and showed her false white teeth. They looked whiter than other people's false teeth, because her face was so yellow and her eyes so dark. Occasionally she flew into an awful temper and swore so dreadfully that it shocked every one who heard her. But at other times she was quite cheerful and told very funny stories.

She had a treacherous friend who was a hunch-backed lady. They both loved the same gentleman, but he couldn't marry them because he had a wife already. The hunch-backed lady used to come in the evening and sit down in the kitchen and say how ill the wife was, and that she couldn't last much longer; but she did. The hunch-backed lady said that as soon as she was dead the gentleman they loved would want to marry the cook, and that he really loved her much better than his wife. The cook believed it, and she said if he had only known his mind when they were young together all the bother would have been saved.

The hunch-backed lady wore a woolly black cloak, and a big fur on her shoulders to hide the hunch, a black velvet bonnet with strings and sparkling jet ornaments, and an expensive gold watch-chain. She had a very heavy face with her chin right on her chest, and light blue eyes and a handsome curly fringe. She used to drink quantities of tea out of a saucer, very hot, but the cook said she really liked whisky much better when she could get it.

Once she ceased coming and the cook went to look for her, and she found out that the wife had really been dead all the while, and the hunch-backed lady had got married to the gentleman they loved. He didn't want to be married, but she made him. She was afraid that if the cook had known his wife was dead *she* would have made him first.

There was a page-boy in this house too, but not an anarchist. He wore no buttons, and he had to stop down in the kitchen and help the cook because of her "poor leg."

She got it through going out to buy three pounds of fish at the fishmonger's and slipping on a piece of orange-peel outside the door. It used to give way just at the most awkward moments, and she said she almost believed it knew and did it on purpose. If she had a saucepan in her hand, or a piece of toast, or a leg of mutton, it was all the same—she had to put it down on the floor and clutch herself round the knee to pull her leg straight again. Everybody knew about it, and the first thing they said when they came into the kitchen was, "Goodmorning, cook, and how's your poor leg?" and then she told them about it. When she sat down the boy used to arrange a chair in front of her for her to rest it on.

He had a fat, red face, and he was always smiling. The cook said she wouldn't have believed that any living mouth could stretch so far. It used to make people angry, because whenever they looked at him he smiled, even when there was nothing at all to smile at. My grandfather said he was like the man in Shakespeare who smiled and was a villain. He liked eating apples and a sweet-stuff called stick-jaw that glued his teeth together. The cook said he was the biggest liar that ever walked the earth. He always pretended he had a serious illness and he must go and see the doctor. But instead he went and played in Regent's Park. Once he tied his face up in a bandage for two days and said that he was going to the dentist to have a double tooth out. And he borrowed a huge cart-horse from one of the stables in the mews and went for a ride on it, without a saddle, and with an old piece of rope instead of reins; and that was how he got found out. The horse insisted on going past the house when it wanted to return to its stable. He tugged at it as hard as he could to make it go home round the back way, but it refused, and the cook was on the area steps and saw him. She said she wouldn't have been so certain if he hadn't had an enormous apple in one hand. When he came next day, he said it was the dentist's horse, and he had sent him for a ride on it to get rid of the effects of laughing gas. But we knew the very stable where it lived, and so he was dismissed.

The housemaid was Irish, and she couldn't read or write, but she believed in ghosts. She had been a long time in the family too, and she was very fat, with a big pink face and little beady eyes. She was the kindest person I ever knew. Whenever we liked anything she had she always wanted to give it to us, and it really grieved her if we wouldn't have it. She gave away all her money to the beggars at the garden gate, and if she heard of any of us being ill or punished it made her cry, just as if she herself were in trouble. She used to fall about a great deal. If there was any place she could fall into she always did. She said she had measured her length upon every free space of ground in the house, and bumped her head on every stair, and caught her foot in every rug and carpet. But she didn't let it worry her. One night, when she was standing on the slippery little knob at the end of the bannisters to light the gas outside the studio door, she fell off and lay quite still with her leg doubled under her until the family had finished dinner, because she didn't want to disturb them by calling out. Once she fell into the drawing-room with a great big tea-tray when there was a tea-party and alarmed the guests exceedingly. But my grandmother was not angry. She said nothing at all, but helped her to get up and pick the tea-things up again.

She believed in ghosts most firmly. She said that her mother had seen so many in Ireland that she simply took no notice of them. They were in every room in the house and up and down the stairs. They used to ring the bells when nothing was wanted and knock people about when they got in their way, and whenever anybody died or anything was going to happen they made a horrible noise outside the windows in the night. Once, she said, she passed a woman nursing her own head on a stone by the roadside, and they just looked at one another, but neither of them spoke.

A gentleman in a nightshirt had hanged himself from a hook in the middle of the ceiling in the servants' bedroom, before my grandfather came to the house, and the housemaid said his spirit haunted the top storey. She woke up one night and saw a figure standing in the middle of the room and looking at her. She knew it was the same gentleman, because he still wore his nightshirt and had the rope round his neck, and he was standing just underneath the place where the hook would have been had it not been taken down when the ceiling was whitewashed. He was looking at her fixedly. If he had looked the other way he might have noticed the cook in the other bed as well, and that would have been some relief. But he didn't. He gazed and gazed as though his heart was going to break. She was so frightened that she shook the bed with trembling; and she shut her eyes and put her hand under the pillow and got out her rosary, and said five "Hail Mary's." And when she opened them again he was still there, only not quite so solid. After another five he had got so misty that she could see the furniture through him, and after the third five he had disappeared. But she was so terrified, she said, that she didn't get a wink of sleep that night, and when she woke in the morning her nightdress and the sheets were quite damp with terror.

The cook didn't believe it. She said it was pure popery. She was sure no ghost could possibly come in in the night like that without her noticing it, because she was such a light sleeper. But as a matter of fact, she snored so dreadfully that my grandfather once asked a builder for an estimate for padding the walls of the servants' room all round so that she couldn't be heard on the floor underneath, but she was so offended that it wasn't padded.

They sometimes used to laugh at the housemaid in the kitchen for being a Catholic. But she didn't care. She stuck to her religion. She was so certain that the Virgin Mary was taking care of her, or she would have been worse hurt in the dreadful accidents she used to have. She said no living being could have stood it without Divine protection. When she was doing something that she thought really might be dangerous, she just said, "Jesus, Mary, Joseph, help!" and took more care, and nothing happened.

The cook said why she didn't like Catholics was because she thought they were wicked for burning the Protestants alive on posts in the streets in the olden days when there were no police. I said that the Protestants burnt the Catholics first, but she was offended. She said that no Protestant would ever have thought of such a thing if it hadn't been put into their heads by bad example. They argued so angrily about which burnt the other first that the housemaid put her apron over her head and sat down on a chair and began to cry aloud like the Irish do at funerals. But then she left off and went upstairs to do her work, and she tumbled about so badly in the bedroom over the studio that my grandfather got down from his painting chair to go upstairs and see what the matter was, and when he found out why she was crying he was very angry. He stumped right downstairs to the top of the kitchen flight with his spectacles on top of his head, his palette in one hand and his paint-brush in the other. It was difficult for him to get downstairs because of his gout. But he did, and put his head over the bannisters and forbade the subject ever again to be mentioned in the kitchen. And it was not, and they were quite good friends again after that.

The person who most hated Catholics was Mrs. Hall, the wife of the most pious cabman in the mews at the corner. She was the beautiful woman who sat in the barge and nursed the healthy baby that had been painted as twins. She was so beautiful that it was quite remarkable. Her hair was jet black, and when one day she sat down in a chair in the kitchen and let it down for us to see it trailed upon the floor. Her eyes were dark blue and extremely big and bright, but the doctor said that the brightness was unnatural, and that later she might go blind. She was very tall, and wherever she stood she used to look strong and composed and like the statues that stand round on pedestals in museums. Her husband used to say God punished her for her sins by not giving her a baby.

The husband went to a chapel where any one who liked could get up and preach, and the others were obliged to listen. He preached every time he got a chance, and he said he never felt inclined to stop. He loved his fellow creatures so much that he felt compelled to save their souls. He always carried a bundle of tracts about in his pocket, and when any one paid him his fare he gave them some free of charge in exchange. My grandfather used to say to him, "It's no good, Hall, I'm past all redemption," because he didn't want the tracts, but Mr. Hall stuffed a bundle into the pocket of his over-coat while he was helping him to get out of the cab. Mrs. Hall said that he wrestled with God for his soul in private. They were allowed to do that at his chapel.

He was so religious that he thought both Catholics and Protestants were wicked. He said the mistake that everybody made was to think there was more than one door open into Heaven. He said, "Is there more than one door open into Heaven? No! And why is there not more than one door open into Heaven? Because if there was more than one door open into Heaven there would be a draught in Heaven. And would the Lord tolerate a draught in Heaven? No!" That was part of one of his sermons. It really meant that it was only the door of his chapel that led into Heaven, and that other people hadn't got a chance.

Some people said he was a handsome man, but I didn't think so. He was small and his hair was such a bright yellow that it looked as if it had been painted. He had strawberry-coloured cheeks and his nose was deadly white. Whenever he met a very nice young girl he used to take her to a prayer-meeting, because he loved her soul. He knew a great many. His wife was angry be-cause he took so much trouble about their souls, and the more he loved them the more she hated them. She used to cry and tell the cook which particular one he was saving then, and the cook used to say, "The sauce hussy! *I'd* save 'er, and 'im too!"

Mrs. Hall cried a lot too, because she hadn't got a baby.

Once when she had been sitting to my grandfather and nursing the baby that had been made into twins for the picture she came into the kitchen, put her head down on the side table where all the dirty dishes were, and cried so bitterly that her shoulders kept heaving up and down, and part of her hair came undone. She said, "It's the feel of it in your arms and then having to give it up again!"

She meant the nice warm wriggly feeling the baby had when we undressed it, because it was so fashionable. I had noticed it too. She said, "If only I'd had one like that I might have kept him."

And the cook said, "Was he out again last night, then?"

And she nodded her head and began to cry worse than before.

The cook was very angry. She said he ought to be ashamed of himself with that nice, beautiful bed and all that any man ought to feel proud and glad to sleep in.

I thought at first she meant the baby, but it was the husband they were speaking of. It was true that he had a beautiful bed, because I once went up into the room over the stable and saw it. It was all hung with white muslin and decorated with big blue bows like a cradle when the baby is a boy. It had a piece of lavender under each pillow (Mrs. Hall lifted them up to show me), and "*Welcome!*" pasted up on the canopy in big gold letters. The room was full of photographs, and they were all of Mr. Hall in different sizes. There was a big black and white picture of him over the mantelpiece, and then they grew smaller and smaller, and the smallest of all was on a chain round Mrs. Hall's neck.

Mr. Hall used to want to save the parlourmaid too, but she didn't want to be saved. She objected so strongly that she said she'd box his ears if he attempted it. So he gave it up.

She was a very tall girl with a big chest and great strong arms. She came from the country. Her skin was something the colour of the paler sort of olives, and her hair was black. Her eyes were a peculiar kind of mixture of dark green and red, and her eyebrows were so thick and dark that they looked like two straight strips of black velvet above her eyes. When she was angry she frowned, and then they joined together and looked like one strip. Her real name was Amelia Parkes, but in the kitchen they called her Milly, and when she had once got to the top of the kitchen stairs she was called Parkes.

She was engaged to marry a horribly cross old green-grocer who lived in Henry Street. She didn't want to, but she said she was obliged to in order not to bring disgrace upon her family. I didn't understand why. She used to cry a great deal about it, so that her eyes were always swollen, but she never let anybody see her cry. She did it in the night.

The man she really loved was called Tommy Haughty. He was the cabman who lived in the last house but one in the mews. He was a huge and friendly young man with dimples and the kindest face imaginable. When we heard a cab come rumbling up the mews we used to say, "I wonder if it's Tommy Haughty," and hope it was, because he always looked so cheerful. When he went past the house he used to stand up on his box and look down the area to see if Milly was in the kitchen, and if she was they used to smile at one another, and then you saw his dimples quite plainly.

But once he stopped coming past the house any more. We used to watch for him, but he always turned his horse the other way and went down Ormonde Terrace. That was after Milly became engaged to the greengrocer. She didn't say anything, but whenever we heard a cab come up the mews she used to turn her back to the window and stand in front of the dresser quite quietly without moving. Once the housemaid went into her bedroom in the night and found her sitting up in bed in the moonlight with her hair hanging down, crying bitterly. She put her arms round her and tried to comfort her, and all Milly said was, "I don't know how I came to do it."

And the housemaid said, "Do you love the other so, then, Milly?"

And she said, "He's been so good to me," and cried worse than before.

The housemaid told my grandfather about it the next morning, and he called Milly into the studio and tried to persuade her not to marry the greengrocer, but she wouldn't listen. He said it's wrong and foolish to marry one man when you love another so badly that you can't sleep for crying. But it had no effect upon her.

So he and the little dog walked down into Henry Street to see the greengrocer and ask him to treat her kindly when they were married. And the old man made his eyes quite narrow and looked him straight in the face and said, "What has it to do with you?" and my grandfather came back and said he was a hardened villain.

One night just before Milly was married Tommy Haughty's mother came to see her in the kitchen, and they quarrelled. She was a little, quick, clean woman, with tiny grey eyes as round as farthings. Her nose turned straight up out of her face and had no bridge at all, and it was quite red at the tip. But she was very tidy.

She said it was all very well to say it was *her* fault, but she was a respectable hard-working widow, and she didn't want her son bringing soiled goods into *their* home. She said he was a lad that any mother might well be proud of, and he'd never spoke a rough word in his life, God bless him, and that though she said it, he was one that could pick and choose where he pleased.

Milly was angry. She told her she wanted nothing to do either with her or her son, and had asked nothing from them. She said, "I'm going to marry the old devil to please myself, so set your mind at rest on *that* score."

Tommy Haughty's mother was so excited that she seemed to keep fizzing up all over her body and simply couldn't be quiet. She said that some people didn't know when they had fallen low enough, and give themselves airs when they ought to be thankful when a respectable married widow wasn't too particular to sit in the same room with them.

Milly kept her temper better. She said, "Go home and tell your son what you've been saying to me if you're not afraid to."

Tommy Haughty's mother fell in a violent temper. She began to talk very loudly, and she said, "I'm not afraid of my son or of an old man's love-light either. If the old fool had got any sense he'd pass you on to the next man willing to take you. And let me tell you this. My son's glad to be well rid of a bad bargain. He says it's lucky he's been spared from taking up another man's leavings."

Then Milly got into a temper too. She stood up and

folded her arms on her chest and pulled her eyebrows together, and said, "You lie, you old beast. Your son would take me now and thankful, if I'd let him."

She looked so tall and angry that Tommy Haughty's mother was afraid. She kept staring at her with her tiny little eyes. They looked as if they were trying to burst out of her head. And Milly said, "Them as tells lies can't believe them as tells the truth, so I'll show you that I'm not a liar like you."

And she put her hand into her bodice and took out a letter and flung it on the table, and said, "There, that's the letter I had from your son this morning."

Tommy Haughty's mother left off staring at Milly and stared at the letter instead. She was awfully surprised and frightened. She put out her hand to take it, but Milly jumped at her and said, "No, don't you touch it. You're not fit to."

And she picked it up and opened it. But then she stood and looked at it without speaking for such a long time that we thought she wasn't going to read it. But at last she did, only not very loudly. It said, "I love you, Milly, just as I did before. You haven't been true to me, Milly, but I've been true to you. If you'll have me now I'll do what's right by you. And I'll do what's right by the child that's coming, Milly. I like the mother and I'll like the child as well. . . ."

She didn't read any more, but there was some more.

57

She kept on standing there, and then she said in a low voice, "I wouldn't have let you hear it, only for the things you'd have said about me afterwards."

She held out the first page of the letter for the cook to see, so that they'd know she had been reading what was really written in it, and then she put it back in her dress again. And she said in the same low voice, "That's how he treats 'soiled goods.'"

Then she was quiet again, and then she said, "I know as well as you do that 'soiled goods' aren't fit for him. Do you think it's *your* dirty tongue that stops me?"

After that they were all quiet for a little time and Tommy Haughty's mother began to fasten up her bonnet strings, and she said, "Well, I'll be going," just as if she'd only come to supper and hadn't been quarrelling at all. And she went away without saying good-night to any one.

The next day I saw Milly at the pillar-box near the house posting a letter. She had on all her nice white frills and apron-strings, and she looked very clean and pretty. She kissed the envelope before she put it in the letter-box, and then she stood still. I ran up to her and said, "Was it for Tommy Haughty, Milly?"

And she said, "Yes, Miss Poppy."

We took hands and walked back towards the house, and I said, "That was why you kissed it, wasn't it,

Milly?" and she didn't answer for a minute, and then she said, "Yes, Miss Poppy."

And I said, "Wouldn't you rather marry Tommy Haughty than that horrid dirty old greengrocer, Milly?"

Then she was silent for such a long time that I thought she wasn't going to answer, but she did and said, "Yes, Miss Poppy."

And after a minute she turned her face away and began to cry and wipe her eyes, and that was the only time that anybody saw her crying in the daytime.

The kitchen was really pleasantest of all in the evening when they were resting after supper. Sometimes there were quite a lot of people there. The charwoman used to unscrew her wooden leg and lean it up against her chair. She said you couldn't think what a relief it gave her. But, of course, if she'd had to get up suddenly for anything before she'd had the time to screw it on again she would certainly have fallen. The cook had her leg up on the chair in front of her and they talked about them. But the charwoman talked most. She was a middle-sized woman with greasy greeny-greyish hair, and there always seemed to be perspiration on her face. She talked whatever she was doing. She talked so much that people could never understand how she got through all the work she did. At first it was disturbing, like rain pattering on a roof, but after a time you wouldn't notice it.

She said that her husband and her husband's mother and her husband's father had all got wooden legs. She said that it was fate, and when the doctor in the hospital had told her that her right must go it was hardly any shock to her. She had a little girl called Sarah, and whenever she had anything the matter with her the first thing she always did with her was to test her legs at once. Even if it was only a cold or something wrong at quite another end of her body she always did. The housemaid said that it was tempting Providence to talk like that, but she didn't care.

She talked most of all with Mrs. Catlin, the woman who did fine needlework and used to make my grandfather's shirts. She was a caretaker in one of the great big houses in Ormonde Terrace, and she used to look so young and innocent that everybody called her the "little woman," when she wasn't there. When she had finished some work she used to bring it round in the evening after her babies were in bed, and then she'd stand near the dresser and talk, but she never sat down round the table with the others. She was rather plump and she always looked pink and clean as though she'd come straight out of a bath. She had nice fluffy fair hair and blue eyes, and her nose turned up just a little at the end, but gently and not suddenly like Tommy Haughty's mother's. She talked a good deal too, but she had a pretty tinkling voice. She said when you'd been shut up in a great big barracks of a place the whole day long you simply must let loose or burst. Sometimes she and the charwoman talked both at once for a long time. They seemed not to hear at all what the other said, but it made no difference. Cook said it was like pandemonium in a hailstorm when those two got together.

The little woman liked to talk about her husband in the lunatic asylum. He had been there three years and she went to see him every week and took him something tasty in a basket. He didn't know her, and it used to make her cry. She said it was like being married to a motherless infant. She thought that lunatics were most peculiar people. She said that one who lived in the asylum where her husband was got up the chimney and was pulled down by the leg, and flung his arms around the nurse's neck, and then walked round the room turning all the pictures with their faces to the wall. She told a very sad story about a poor man who had been sent for to clean the windows of the asylum, and when he looked through into the room he could see his own wife sitting melancholy-mad in an armchair. The tears rolled down his face when he saw her, and he might have fallen off the ladder, and if he had there would have been a whole family of little children left fatherless; but he didn't. The woman used to sit all day long in an armchair, staring at the fire and taking no notice of anything, and when anybody spoke to her she used to look up and say, "Eh? Oh, yes," and then go on staring at the fire again. When they brought her little new baby to see her she just stroked its cheek and smiled, but she didn't know who it was and wouldn't make friends, and just looked at the fire again. But at last, one day, she suddenly noticed the nurse making a bed, and all of a sudden she got up and said, "Oh, nurse, how lazy of me to be sitting here doing nothing and you with all that work to do." And she helped her make the bed and went on doing lots of other work, and the doctors said she was cured, and she went home to her husband and children. The little woman cried when she told the story, and said it was the thought of them blessed innocents in their mother's arms again. She was very tender-hearted.

The cook used to say to her, "And how's the policeman, Mrs. Catlin?"

And she used to blush and say, "Now, cook, don't, now!"

I knew the policeman they meant. He was a big and handsome policeman, and I saw him handing parcels to her down the area in Ormonde Terrace. She looked like a clean, rosy apple in a coal-scuttle, in the bottom of the big, dark area.

One night when they were teasing her because the policeman was so loving she nearly cried and said, "Well, now, can you blame me, now? He's that kind to my children, and it's that lonely in that great big gloomy barracks of a night——"

And then suddenly she stopped short as if she oughtn't to have said it, and looked ashamed, and nobody spoke till the cook said, "Well, Mrs. Catlin, so it's come to that then!"

And Mrs. Hall was offended, but I didn't know why. But the others laughed and the little woman held her head down.

Then the husband died and she married the policeman, and not long afterwards she came to see us all dressed in black crepe and with a nice new baby in her arms. She cried a great deal about her husband, but she adored the baby. It really belonged to the policeman, but I didn't ask where he had kept it up till then.

❦❦❦

Not long after that something so terrible happened that I think I shall never forget it as long as I live. My dear grandfather died. He had only been ill a few days, and his illness began on the very night he finished the big picture. There was a nurse in uniform in the house and doctors drove up to the door in carriages. They wouldn't let me see him, though I begged to be allowed to, and the nurse said that he probably would not know me. But

I could not believe that, I was sure she said it only because she didn't want to let me in. I used to wait outside the door because I thought I might be able to slip in when she wasn't looking, and I felt certain that if once he only saw me there he would never let them turn me out again. But one night when the nurse went downstairs for something I slipped up the stairs to his bedroom door. I listened for a moment outside, but I could hear nothing. Then I turned the handle very gently and went in.

He was lying in the bed and there was a lamp burning on the table near him. He lay so still that at first I thought it must be a stranger there, and I was afraid and felt inclined to run away. But then I saw his hand twitch slightly and I wasn't afraid any longer.

I crept up to the bed and looked at him. I didn't wish to wake him, but I was so eager to see him. He was lying on his back with the clothes right up to his chin, and his beard was spread out over the sheet. His hands were folded on his chest.

His face looked intensely proud and lonely. It seemed to have changed somehow, and to be made of some cold and hard material, with deep new lines carved all over it. His white hair was spread out on the pillow and, as I looked at him, I remembered the picture of a great, stern snow-mountain lying all alone that he had once shown me.

I was going to creep away again because I was afraid

of waking him, but all of a sudden he turned his head towards me and opened his eyes and looked at me. It startled me, because he did it so quickly and quietly and I didn't expect it. But I was glad, and I said, "Grandpapa."

But he went on looking at me as though he didn't see me, and he didn't smile. And suddenly he said quite quietly, "I'm sorry, I don't know you," just as coldly and politely as if I had been a grown-up visitor come to look at the pictures, and he turned his head away.

But I said, "Grandpapa," again. I felt I was going to cry, but I didn't, and he turned round and smiled just a little and said, "Ah, little pigeon."

But then he turned his head away and forgot again.

I stood quite still. I felt dreadfully unhappy. It was the first time in my life that he hadn't seemed glad to see me. I felt that it would kill me if he didn't say one kind, loving word to me. It was terribly lonely. The wind was howling outside, but it was quite quiet inside the room.

Then my grandfather said, without turning his head, "The Guy Fawkes boys were making just such a noise outside the windows as they're doing now on the night when your brother Oliver died."

And then he began to say,

Please to remember
The fifth of November . . .

And then he laughed a little, very low, a peculiar dreadful laugh, as if he didn't know that he was laughing. And I said, "Grandpapa, my Oliver isn't dead at all. It was your own boy Oliver who died on Guy Fawkes' night."

I felt again that I was going to cry, because he was making such a strange mistake and because he laughed like that. I knew it was his own boy who died on Guy Fawkes' night because my mother had often told me the story.

He had loved his son Oliver so intensely that he had never forgotten him for a moment since his death. It made it all the worse because he would not believe at first that his boy was ill and said that he was lazy. And after he was dead they found a number of medicine bottles in his cupboard, and discovered that he had been trying to cure himself alone. But it was no use.

My grandfather kept all the pictures he had painted and all the books he liked to read in a little room next his own, and it was called "Oliver's room." He had the key in his pocket, and he used to go in all alone and touch the things and look at them. Sometimes he took my hand and let me go in with him.

When they were going to bury his boy and all the carriages were waiting, he called my mother and my grandmother to him and forbade them to shed a single tear.

He said, "This is the funeral of my son and not a puppet-show."

And they were so frightened because he looked so stern and dreadful that they dared not cry, and my grandmother trembled so that my mother had to put her arm round her to hold her up. And he walked down-stairs to where all the people were waiting with his head straight up as if he cared nothing. But it was really be-cause, if he had heard Oliver's mother crying at his grave it would have sent him mad.

But it was all so long ago I thought perhaps he had forgotten, and I said, "Grandpapa, don't you remember that it was your own boy who died on Guy Fawkes' night?"

And then he turned his face right round again and looked at me. And this time he smiled his own old smile, but the one that made his eyes look sad, and his face seemed somehow to melt a little and turn into soft, rosy flesh again. And he said, "My own boy?"

And he kept on looking at me and smiling kindly just as he used to do when I said something that pleased him very much. And I felt very happy. I was just going to say, "Grandpapa, do you feel well now?" when all of a sud-den his face seemed to die away and grow hard again, and he turned his head away and forgot. And I could hear him saying very low,

Please to remember
The fifth of November . . .

And then he went to sleep and didn't move again. I waited a little, and then I crept out of the room and went downstairs and cried because he had not really been glad to see me.

And one night, a little while after that, the doctor was sent for and people kept running up and down the stairs and everybody looked frightened. The cook was sitting in the hall crying because some newspaper reporters kept ringing at the bell to know if F. M. B. had passed away yet, and one of them offered her five shillings secretly if she would tell him before the others.

My grandfather was dead. Next day when I went out I saw on the placards, "Death of F. M. B.," and I stood and stared at them. I didn't cry because I couldn't believe that the dead man was really my dear grandpapa, who had always been there in the studio winding himself up and down in the screw-chair, and calling me "little pigeon," and loving me. It seemed to me somehow that even the newspaper boards would pity me and say something kind to me if it were really he, and not look so dead and hard as if they cared nothing for either of us.

But when I went back again, and the studio was empty, and the screw-chair was turned round to the ladder just as he had left it when he last climbed down, and his cap and spectacles were lying on the table where he had put them that night when my mother helped him upstairs to bed because he was so tired, and he had said to her, "Well, my dear, my work's done now"—then I cried.

CHAPTER THREE

The Convent

Soon after my grandfather was dead I went to school in a convent. I had some relations who were Roman Catholics, and they were very pious. They were so religious that they believed that every child who wasn't baptised in the proper way would go to hell and burn for all eternity when it was dead. They didn't wish me to be burnt like that, although they really didn't know me very well. They thought I might have a chance of being properly baptised and going to heaven if I went to school in a convent. And so I did.

It was a big red building with a number of windows and a green square in front of it. It had an arched door like a church door with a nicely polished brass plate in the middle with the name of the convent on it in black letters. The bell hung down at the side on a chain, and just above the brass plate there was a little square grating with a tiny window behind it. When anybody rang the bell a nun opened the window and looked through the grating to see if it was a respectable person ringing. If it was, she opened the door; but if it was a person who didn't look respectable, like a thief or somebody with a bad character, she went to ask permission before she let them in.

Inside the door was a wide corridor with a tiled floor and windows on both sides, and on the right a big door that opened into the chapel. The corridor led into other corridors, and large class-rooms opened out of them on either side filled with desks and maps and pictures. Upstairs there were more corridors with tiny bedrooms for the boarders opening out of them. In each room there was a crucifix over the bed and a shell full of holy water. When the nun came to wake you in the morning she stood by the bed and held out the shell of holy water, and (if you weren't a heretic) you were supposed to dip your fingers into the water and make the sign of the cross to show that you were thoroughly awake. If you were a heretic, she simply said "Good Morning." When you got out of bed another nun came in and brushed and combed your hair. That part was the same whether you were a heretic or not, but if you weren't you went into the chapel to hear mass as soon as you'd finished breakfast.

The chapel was very pretty with a quantity of blue

and gold paint about it. There was a statue of the Virgin Mary on the right-hand side of the altar, and she was in blue and gold as well. She had a pink-and-white looking face, and her eyes were made of glass, like a doll's. She wore a blue dress and a gold crown in her hair and held a dear, loving little baby in her arms, with a blue frock and gold hair. She appeared to take no notice of it, but stared straight in front of her with her eyebrows lifted as if she were extremely surprised at something. St. Joseph, her husband, was standing on the other side of the altar in a handsome blue gown all covered over with golden stars, and held a golden crook in his hand. His eyes were brown, and he didn't look so surprised as the Virgin Mary—only dogged. There were some other saints round the sides of the chapel, but they weren't nearly so well dressed.

Over the altar there was a beautiful portrait of Mary Magdalene, who was wicked once but got better later on. She had on a blue dress too, and her hair was golden, but not tidily kept like the Virgin Mary's. It fell down all round her right to her feet and looked as bright as if it had just been washed and combed out. Her face was pale and sad and lovely. I liked her better than the Virgin Mary. I thought she looked as if she had a much better character. But, of course, she hadn't. She was very bad until she was converted, and then she tied her hair up and was sorry for her sins.

There was a big crucifix in the chapel, and a long picture of the twelve apostles all standing in a row with their feet in sandals and on clouds. They had brown dresses on and ropes round their waists, and gold halos on the back of their heads to show how saintly they were. Their faces were nearly all painted alike, except for hairdressing, because there were no pictures or photographs in those days to go by, but if you wanted to know which was which you looked at their names, which were written in gold letters underneath the clouds.

There were a lot of big, expensive candles on the altar to show respect to God, and down near the altar rails there was a sort of upright candelabra with spikes all over it for sticking smaller candles on. A pile of candles lay near. Some cost a halfpenny, and some cost a penny, and there was a money-box on a little table for you to put the money in to pay for them. (It's the same in all Catholic churches, because it is thought that candles are so much appreciated in heaven.) You light a candle and stick it on the candelabra with a special prayer to the Virgin Mary or one of the saints for something you really want. You light a halfpenny candle if it's an easy thing and a penny one if you feel you're going rather far. It's a little more expensive, but it's worth it. The Virgin Mary sometimes grants a request for nothing, but she's much more likely to do it if you light a candle. So are the saints. It's a special way to please them.

In the middle of the altar was a kind of little square house called the Tabernacle in which the Sacred Host was kept. It was extremely holy. Everybody who passed it had to bend the knee in adoration, and the sacristan kept it nicely dusted with a feather brush.

On the right hand of the chapel near the sacristy door was a big, upright box like an open wardrobe, with an arch on the top and curtains across the front and a little place behind curtains to kneel on at either side. That was the confessional. Catholics go to confession and get their sins forgiven about once a week, generally on Saturday night, so that they won't have time to commit any more sins (especially if they go to bed at once) before seven o'clock on Sunday morning when they go to communion. The safest time to sin is on Friday and on Saturday morning and afternoon and early on Saturday evening, so that there is not so much chance of dying and going to hell between the sinning and going to confession.

The priest sits in the middle of the confessional behind the curtains and forgives sins quite easily, and when he has forgiven them God does. But if you die in mortal sin before the priest forgives you, you go to hell and burn for all eternity, and when you're once there no power on earth can ever get you out again. Hell is a great burning pit full of flames and red-hot cinders where the devils live. They are used to the heat and go about their business just as usual, but Catholics who die in mortal sin and go there never get to like it. That's their punishment. Mortal sin is a sin that's really dreadful, such as coming late to mass on Sunday, eating meat on Friday, or murdering your father and mother. There's another kind of sin that's not so bad, called venial sin, such as cheating or fighting or being unkind to one another. If you die in that sort of sin you go to purgatory.

Purgatory is not so frightful as hell because it's not kept so hot, and if you are patient there and don't complain your sins are forgiven after some time, and you go to heaven just as usual. But, of course, it's pleasanter and shorter to go to confession just before you die, so that you don't have time to go wrong again.

There's another way of keeping out of purgatory in advance, but you must be able to count well to do it. It's by saying special sort of prayers called "indulgenced prayers." Every time you say them some of the purgatory that you've been letting yourself in for is knocked off. Some knock off forty days, some sixty and some more, so that if you can say them quickly enough you can get rid of a year in no time. But, of course, you must keep count as you go along or it's pure waste of prayers, and it's very difficult to count properly unless you're used to it. The best thing is to have a pencil and a piece of paper in front of you while you pray and jot it down, though some people are very clever at counting on their fingers. There are some quite special prayers that knock off all purgatory at one blow. They are much longer than the others, but I always thought they saved time in the end, and they are much safer.

There's another place called "Limbo," kept at quite a mild temperature, where the souls of the people who died before Our Lord came to save the world are detained. They long to go to heaven but they can't, however good they've been, because they lived before the forgiveness of sins was established. If they went straight to heaven there would be no knowing whose sins had been forgiven and whose had not, and it would cause great confusion, so they have to wait till the last day, when every one will get what they deserve. It's very sad, but it can't be helped.

Hell, purgatory and limbo, seem to be like three separate compartments—hot, hotter, and hottest—with the lids on, and they all want looking after. It sounds puzzling until you've learnt about it in the catechism, but it is really quite simple, and with the grace of God all will come right in the end. On the last day, when the deafening trumpet has been sounded, purgatory and limbo will both be emptied and the people in them will be admitted into heaven; but hell will go on for ever and ever to satisfy the wrath of God.

When I first went to the convent I hadn't been baptised at all, not even in an improper way, and every one was sorry for me, as if I had measles or some bad illness.

The nuns used to say, "Don't you know that you are not the child of God?" or, "Don't you think it would be dreadful if you died in the night and suddenly found yourself in a pit of awful fire?"

I said, yes, I did think it would be dreadful. And so I did. But at the same time I didn't want to be baptised because no one had ever before told me that it would be so good for me. I was so obstinate that one of the nuns who was very kind-hearted used nearly to begin to cry whenever she looked at me, and she couldn't sleep at night for praying that I might be converted. I thought it very kind of her, because she was no relation. The girls used to tell me too that I should go to hell, but I didn't care at all for what they said. They were not severely dressed in black and white with long rosaries round their waists as the nuns were. The thing was that I didn't really believe in hell. I thought if it was true it would have been in all the papers and I should have heard about it somehow. But I sometimes used to feel uncomfortable and think it might be better to be on the safe side.

The person who talked to me about it most of all was Reverend Mother, and I was more frightened of her than of anybody else. She always seemed so much grander and more important than any of the other nuns. The black part of her dress seemed blacker, and the white part whiter, and her rosary heavier and longer than theirs, but that was only because she was the Reverend Mother. She was very big and broad, and her skirts waved to and fro so that they almost touched the walls on each side of the corridor as she walked along. Her face was light brown and quite square, like a piece of cardboard, and her eyes were round and dark and bright. The mouth was so long that the ends of it seemed to get lost in each side of her coif, and her teeth were big and yellow. Everybody was afraid of her, because she was so holy and had such a deep loud voice. When she came into the class-rooms to listen to the lessons the girls trembled. Sometimes she used to interrupt and ask a question herself, but it was nearly always one of three questions: first, the sons and character of William the Conqueror; second, a list of the seven capital sins or vices and their contrary virtues; and third, the French for Father, Son, and Holy Ghost. When she prayed she looked so severe I thought the saints must feel alarmed.

One day she sent for me into her private room where she received visitors and scared naughty girls and invented punishments. She was sitting in her great armchair waiting for me. I stood in front of her, but I was afraid to look at her face, so I looked at her hands. They were lying in her lap with black mittens on. They looked immensely strong and heavy.

She said she had sent for me because she had something to say to me—did I understand? And I said, "Yes, Reverend Mother."

And then she asked me whether I had made up my mind to become one of God's children by being received by baptism into the Catholic church.

I was dreadfully frightened, but I hadn't made up my mind, so I said, "No, Reverend Mother."

Then she said, did I know that God couldn't possibly love me until I had been baptised, and I said, "Yes, Reverend Mother."

She said, did I want to remain for ever an outcast from the community of the blessed, and I was just going to say, "Yes, Reverend Mother," but I thought perhaps that wasn't the right answer, and I said, "No, Reverend Mother," and that was right.

Then she told me she had had a vision. She said she had seen the souls of two little children before the judgment seat of God. One soul was white as snow, but the other had a large ugly stain on it as black as ink. That was because it had never been cleansed by baptism. The little white soul was let into heaven, and God and all the saints and angels rejoiced, but the little black soul was cast forth into hell, and God and all the saints and angels were full of sorrow.

That was the end of the story. I thought it was a fool-ish story. The child with the black soul couldn't help that it had not been baptised, and God could surely just for once have let the little soul into heaven if He was really grieved about it. But I didn't dare to say so. I said nothing at all, but my face grew hot and I stared at the floor and twisted my fingers together and looked sulky and stupid. Then Reverend Mother said, would nothing ever touch my heart, and had I got nothing to say to her? I daren't go on being silent as if I wasn't interested, but my head went round and I could think of nothing to say. Then I remembered something just in time. I asked was there a kitchen stove in hell?

Reverend Mother looked surprised and shocked. She said no cooking would be done in hell, at least no cook-ing of food; that the souls of the damned would hunger and thirst for ever.

I said I didn't mean that; but there had been a big kitchen stove in the kitchen of my grandfather's house, and I had once tripped up and fallen with my hands straight on it when it was nearly red-hot.

That was true, and I had never forgotten how terribly it had burnt my hands and what awful blisters I had had. When I told Reverend Mother about it I remembered how kind my grandfather had been when I showed him my hands, and how he had loved me. I was afraid I was going to cry, but I didn't want her to see. I was so sinful that I nearly hated her.

She said she didn't know about a kitchen stove in hell, but that each of the damned would certainly find there the thing that he most feared and hated. That was part of the plan.

Then she told me to go and think over all that she had said. She hoped that if nothing else could influence me the fear of hell might lead me to the love of God. My eyes were so full of tears that I could hardly see my way to the door, but I got out of the room without her noticing it. When I was outside in the corridor I put my arm up against the wall and hid my face and cried, because I wanted so much to see my grandfather. I knew he would have comforted me and said that all she had told me was not true. Then I heard some soft footsteps and a rustling sound near me, and when I looked up I saw some nuns coming in procession from the refectory. They looked wonderfully clean and saintly, and they moved so quietly and smoothly that you could hardly hear them.

When they saw me crying they stopped and came round me and tried to comfort me. They said, what a silly little girl to cry when so many of God's greatest blessings were within her reach. There were so many little girls who had not the great chances I had of being called to grace. One of the nuns, the one I loved best of all, called Sister L., held my hand and took me to a window seat and sat down and asked me what was the matter. I said I had been with Reverend Mother and she put her arm round me and drew me up against her, although the nuns were forbidden ever to kiss or embrace the children, and she said, "God loves all little children. He has made them Himself so helpless and innocent."

Her dress and veil felt soft and holy. When they touched me it was like being caressed by something pure and tender. I was so wicked that I felt ashamed to stand so near her. I was afraid that if everything religious people said was true she might be sent to hell for saying that God loved all children, even if they weren't Catholics.

I said, "I'm not frightened, but I hate her."

And she said, "Oh, hush!" and got up and glided away down the corridor so silently that I couldn't hear her move at all. She didn't once look back, and I knew it was because she was so shocked that I could be wicked enough to hate Reverend Mother; and I began to cry again.

I continued to be wicked. I didn't love God and I didn't believe in hell. I was quite sure that if my grandfather had been told about children being burnt in hell he would have said that it was nonsense and that I needn't believe it.

But one day I tumbled into a puddle in the playground and was sent down to dry my clothes in front of the kitchen fire. I had never been in the kitchen before. It was a big kitchen with a stove in it larger than any stove I had ever seen. There were great iron bars across the front of it and the fire was blazing and roaring behind them. The middle bar was quite red-hot and, as I stood there, the heat scorched my face and hands. I thought how terribly it would hurt to have one's hands tied down on to that red-hot bar so that one could never get them off again. It made me feel quite faint to think about it, and then I remembered that if it were true about hell, hell might be just like that stove with fire blazing and roaring, and that all the people who weren't Catholics might go there and be tied on to red-hot bars. Suddenly I thought, what if it's true? and I was frightened. I was so frightened that I determined to be a Catholic straight away. I nearly ran straight to Reverend Mother's room to tell her so, but I was afraid of that as well. So I stopped in front of the fire and kept saying to myself, "It *isn't* true." But in the night I woke up and remembered the stove and I was terrified again, and next morning I told the nuns that I wanted to be baptised and they were very glad. They seemed just as happy and excited as if some-body had given them a beautiful present. They smiled at me and congratulated me and held a service in the chapel to thank God for my conversion. Everybody looked bright and cheerful the whole day long, and all were kind and affectionate and said special prayers for me. We had an extra hour for recreation that evening, and Reverend Mother came to us in the middle of it and brought me a nice new prayer-book and a pretty picture-card of the Holy Ghost descending upon the Apostles. She said she would thank God night and day for having listened to her prayers and touched my heart and converted me. But it wasn't really God who had converted me. It was the kitchen stove.

I Am Baptised

Not long after I was converted I was received into the Catholic church. But I needed a great deal of instruction first, because my soul was so utterly dark. I began by learning the catechism.

The catechism says that everybody is responsible for Adam's sin of greediness when he ate the apple which the Lord specially wanted kept. Adam didn't really care so very much for apples, but his wife tempted him to eat it. We all bear the stain of his guilt upon our souls, because he was the first man created, and it's his fault that there are so many people on the earth to sin against the Lord, because he would go on having so many children and grandchildren. The Blessed Virgin is the only person who isn't blamed for Adam's sin, because she really had nothing to do with it. When I heard about it I was very glad I was going to be baptised and have my sins forgiven because, I thought, what with my own sins and what with Adam's things would be very difficult for me, and I needed all the grace I could possibly get. I was afraid at first that I shouldn't be able to believe about Adam, but then I thought that if I was going to be a Catholic I'd better get used to believing things. So I believed.

I liked being baptised. I wore a pretty white muslin dress with a pale blue sash, and a wreath of flowers and a lace veil on my head, and white gloves and shoes and stockings. It suited me beautifully. I couldn't see myself because no looking-glasses were allowed in the convent, but when I came down dressed all the girls wanted to be the first to kiss me, because they said I looked so sweet.

Everybody gave me presents. Some gave me prayer-books, and some gave me little statues of the saints, and some gave me picture-cards. One of the nuns gave me a rosary blessed by the Pope, and Reverend Mother gave me an Agnus Dei, a round piece of wax with the picture of a lamb stamped on it, sewn up in a bag with strings so that I could hang it round my neck. Catholics are delighted to get an Agnus Dei, because it's a most sacred thing, blessed by the Pope, and when you wear it the devil gets discouraged about you.

The Pope is a very holy man. He blesses things for nothing, and he is infallible. That means that he cannot err when he is teaching people what to believe and how to please God. He really *knows* what he is talking about. And if only people would not be so obstinate, but would believe everything he tells them without arguing, they wouldn't slaughter one another and quarrel about the proper way to be saved. I found that difficult to believe also when I first learnt it in the catechism, but then I tried hard and succeeded.

I was baptised in the Catholic church at the end of the square not far from the convent. The girls and nuns walked behind me in procession, and Reverend Mother walked in front of me, first of all. She looked very proud and important and folded her hands in her sleeves, and her dress waved backwards and forwards across the pavement.

When we got to the church a young priest called Father A. was waiting to baptise me. I knew him, because he used to come to the convent in the morning to say mass in the chapel. He was a good and holy priest, extremely tall and pale and as thin and quiet as a shadow. There were deep hollows under his cheek-bones, and his eyes were sunk so far back and hidden in such dark shadows that you could scarcely ever see them distinctly, even in broad daylight. His lips were always moving in prayer. He walked very fast, with long steps, and even in the street he prayed as he went along, and whenever he passed the church he stood still on the pavement and bowed his head and crossed himself, and paid no attention when rude little boys were surprised and laughed at him. He often stood in front of the crucifix at the bottom of the church praying with his head bent down, and if you went near enough you could see that his shoulders were shaking and tears were running down his cheeks. That was because he was so sorry for Christ that he had been scourged and crucified.

He was thin because he gave nearly all his food to the poor and ate nothing but dry bread. He gave away his clothes as well and never wore an overcoat even in winter, and he slept on the floor because he had given away his bed. But he was most terribly severe to sinners, and many people daren't go to confess to him because he scared them so and gave them such dreadful penances. He scourged and tortured himself that he might never forget the pain our Lord had felt, and soon after I was baptised he went away to nurse the lepers, because he thought his life was still too easy and he wanted to see nothing but pain and misery till he died. He thought that was the right way to comfort Our Lord and help Him to forget what He had suffered.

When we got into the church he was standing near the font, waiting, in his cassock. It was as white as snow and he was praying to himself with his hands folded in his sleeves and his eyes quite hidden in shadows. Reverend

Mother took off my veil and wreath, and I went and stood in front of him. I felt afraid as though I were standing near to God.

He put his hands on my head and blessed me, and then stood quite still and silent, but I could see that his lips were moving. His hands were so thin and light that I could scarcely feel them on my head; but they smelled beautiful. He must have washed them with scented soap to get them clean enough to touch the holy water with.

He went on praying for a long time, but he made no sound, and the shadows round his eyes seemed to get blacker and blacker. The nuns and children fell on their knees round the font, and it was perfectly silent. For a moment I felt afraid, but I didn't move, and all of a sudden he bent down to me and said, quite low, "Oh, my little child, love Christ. He bled for you. He died for you. It is in the love of little ones like you that He finds comfort."

His voice shook so that I thought he was crying, and so he was. When I looked up in his face I saw tears on his cheeks.

Then he sprinkled holy water on my head and said the words of baptism that made God free to love me.

I was glad to be baptised and get my sins forgiven, but I wished I knew whether my grandfather and all the people I had loved before had been baptised too. I thought how dreadful it would be if I went to heaven and found they were not there. But then I remembered that if I could approach God, Himself, one day in heaven when Reverend Mother was not near I could tell Him what good people they really were, and beg Him to let them in. If I could once get near to God I needn't be afraid of Reverend Mother.

My First Confession

I needed more special instruction before I made my first confession. Everybody does; but I was given more than others, because I wasn't used to believing things and required so many explanations. The nuns said that was because I had been so shockingly brought up.

It says in the catechism that the real way to repent of your sins when you go to confession is to be sorry for them only because they have offended God, and not because you have deserved hell by them. I was afraid that I shouldn't be able to be sorry in the right way when the time came. I used to practise, but I found it very difficult. I didn't regret offending God half as much as going to hell. I didn't feel I knew God very well; but if I had not had to think so much about escaping hell I might have been sorry for offending Him. I had not time enough for both.

I made my first confession in a black dress and a black

lace veil to a priest in the convent chapel. I was to have made it to a very kind priest, Father W., but he was taken ill with gout and couldn't come.

Father W. was a dear old man, quite different from Father A., and he had the gout in his feet so badly that it took him quite a long time to hobble down the square from the church to the convent, but he only laughed and said it was a just punishment for his sins. He had a very handsome, saintly face. It looked as delicate and fragile as an egg-shell, but it had a quantity of tiny lines all over it, because he was very old. He had white hair falling nearly to his shoulders and golden-brown eyes which looked at you so kindly that you longed for him to bless you. Children came running from all sides for him to bless them when he walked down the square, even Protestant children.

People said that he had visions. They said that once a ghostly nun came and sat at the foot of his bed and told him what it would be like in heaven. Sometimes he came into the playground when we were having recreation and then the smaller children would run to him and pull him down on to a seat and climb on his knee or lean against him and say, "What did the nun tell you about heaven, Father?" And he would smile and shake his head and say, "Little mice mustn't be too fond of gobbling cheese. Little children mustn't be too fond of asking questions." And his eyes would grow misty as though with tears, and he'd say, "The heart of man hath not conceived the joys God hath prepared for them that love Him." And he'd put his hands on our heads and look lovingly at us and say, "God has prepared a special place for each of His little ones, a special nest for each of His fledglings."

He was very fond of us. He never told us about the horrors of hell, but always about the joy of heaven. When we asked him about hell he always said, "Never mind about that, my chickens. The devil is not so black as he's painted." And if we insisted he would say, "God loves us all. Every hair of our heads is precious to Him. Can we not trust ourselves into His keeping?"

When it was a fine evening and he wanted us to stay out longer at recreation he used to say to the nuns, "Let them enjoy themselves. I'll put it right with the Blessed Virgin. She and I understand one another." He talked about God and the saints as though he really knew them. People said he imposed very easy penances at confession, and forgave your sins almost before you had finished confessing them.

One day, about four in the afternoon, Reverend Mother came into the refectory when we were having tea and said the priest had come to hear my confession. I felt dreadfully nervous. I put on my black veil and fetched my prayer-book. Reverend Mother took my hand, and we went into the chapel. There was no one there at all, but there was a dim light over everything and a smell of incense, and a still and holy feeling.

Reverend Mother told me to go and kneel at the prie-Dieu near the confessional, and prepare myself for confession, and I went on tip-toe and knelt there. My knees were trembling so I feared I should topple over. I tried to pray, but my head was giddy and I didn't know what I was saying. Reverend Mother was kneeling in a seat two or three rows behind me, and that made it all the worse. Then I heard the chapel door open, and the priest walked up the chapel and squeezed himself into the confessional and pulled the curtain across the front of it. I knew he'd have to squeeze himself in because he was so fat. He had a heavy, greasy face and a large Roman nose that always seemed to jut up in the air, and his cheeks were so puffy that his eyes looked like little slits above them. He was new at the church and hadn't spoken to any of us yet.

You take about a quarter of an hour to prepare yourself for confession. That gives you about five minutes to remember your sins and ten minutes to be sorry for them; or you can do it the other way round if you like. I had examined my conscience the night before in bed, and had learnt my sins by heart, so I had an extra five minutes for repenting.

I kept repeating, "Oh, my God, I am sorry for my

sins, and not because I fear the pains of hell," but I knew quite well it was not true. I really was not very sorry, and I did fear the pains of hell, very much indeed. My heart began to beat harder because I was so anxious. I knew that time was passing, and that if I did not repent quickly I should not make a good confession. I continued saying to God, "I am sorry," but every minute I grew more and more afraid knowing that I should soon be obliged to rise and go into the confessional. I thought that when I stood up I should certainly fall, because my legs felt so weak. At last I gave up trying to repent and felt nothing but fear. Then Reverend Mother came up behind and touched me on the shoulder and I nearly screamed, because she had moved so quietly that I thought it was a ghost.

She said, "It's time."

And I got up and nearly tumbled through the curtain into the confessional.

At first it seemed quite dark inside. There was a wire grating between me and the priest, and I could only just see a mass of something white behind it. At first I didn't know what it was and I was afraid to go near, but then it moved and I could see that it was the priest's cassock.

I knelt down on the stool and stared through the grating. I felt that if I were to take my eyes away for one moment the white thing would jump out and seize me. I was shaking all over and the wooden stool seemed to cut into my knees, but I dug my finger-nails into the ledge in front of me and tried to keep still.

The white thing moved again and the priest turned round to my side of the confessional. I could see a big pale lump where his face was, and I felt that his tiny eyes were staring in my direction. I dug my finger-nails still harder into the wooden ledge. If only he had said something it would have been better; but he didn't. He was waiting for me to begin.

I said the first part of the "confiteor" almost unconsciously.

It's a long prayer you say at confession to remind God and the Virgin Mary and St. Michael the Archangel and John the Baptist and the Blessed Apostles Peter and Paul, and several of the other saints, that you are going to confess, so that they may get ready to listen. When you come to the middle you stop to get breath and name your sins.

I was so nervous that I could only feel my lips moving and didn't know in the least what I was saying. But I had learnt it so carefully by heart, and practised it so often, that I got through it without any mistakes and struck my breast properly three times when I came to "through my fault, through my fault, through my most grievous fault."

I was very pleased that I had managed it so well. I almost forgot to name my sins, because I was so pleased and surprised. But then I remembered and did.

When I had counted them up on my fingers the night before they came to four; but now, of course, I had to add about not loving God and not being sorry for my sins, and that made six.

Some were bad ones, such as being unbelieving. That's one of the worst sins. I didn't believe about the devil's climbing over the fence into the Garden of Eden, and disguising himself as a serpent and making all the trouble about the apple. I thought it more likely that Eve wanted the apple from the very beginning and invented the story about the serpent in order to put the blame on the devil. He had such a bad character already that anything would have been believed against him. I didn't believe either about the whale's being seasick and casting up Jonah on to dry land all tidily dressed as though nothing had happened as he appears in Bible pictures. I didn't believe that all the animals walked into the ark two and two, and behaved properly when Noah explained to them about the flood. I was sure some of them would have quarrelled.

Those were really three sins, but I put them all together and called them *heresy*. Then there was *frivolity*, because I had laughed one morning during mass when the boy who was serving slipped down the altar steps and sat on the floor. Then there was *gluttony*, because I had sucked an acid-drop one morning during the catechism lesson. It made rather few sins, but I couldn't think of any more. I hadn't stolen anything or told lies or been rude to any one. I wished I had, because I was afraid that perhaps the priest might think it hadn't been worth while to come on purpose to forgive so few sins. It seemed like sending things to the wash when they're not properly dirty. But as the sins of heresy and impenitence were really bad I thought perhaps it would be all right.

I confessed sins of heresy and frivolity and gluttony, and then I said that I didn't really love God and that I wasn't properly sorry for my sins, and the priest was dreadfully startled. I knew he was because I heard him wriggle all over and he said, quite sharply, "Eh?"

I told him again, and he said that *impenitence* was the most deadly of all sins, and that without penitence no absolution could be given.

I felt very distressed because I had come on purpose to get absolution, and I didn't know what to say. And he said, "Doesn't the fear of everlasting hell lead you to repent your sins and vices?"

I said, yes, but I didn't think that was sufficient; and he said, by heart, out of the catechism, "Sorrow for sins because by them we have lost heaven and deserved hell is sufficient when we go to confession. Don't you learn your catechism?"

I said, yes, but I had got it confused somehow. I was very relieved, and I thought how stupid I had been wasting so much time in trying to be sorry because I had offended God when I really need not have bothered. It made things so much easier.

He took no notice about my not loving God, and he said, "Have you no more sins to confess?" I didn't wish to seem proud, so I said there might be, but I couldn't remember them at the moment. And then he said, "Had I been guilty of pride, covetousness, or lust?"

I wasn't quite sure what they meant, though I had had most sins properly explained. (I was very stupid at understanding about religious things.) I thought it might sound like boasting if I said, no, so I said, "Yes, Father."

And he said, "Rage or slander?"

And I said, "Yes, Father."

And he said, "Presumption, sloth, malice, or avarice, parsimony, the desires of the flesh?"

And I said, "Yes, Father."

He said the sins just as though he were counting them up on his fingers, and not at all in an interested manner or as though he really cared whether I had committed them or not.

I had no notion what the last two meant, but I thought

that I might have been guilty of them without knowing it, and that I had better have them all forgiven while I had a chance. (One can't be too careful).

Then the priest gave me a lecture. It sounded as though it were said by heart, but it was not, really. He made it up as he went along. He explained why we had to avoid each of those sins and why they offended God. There were so many that it took him quite a long time, and I couldn't understand many of the words he used. I tried to at first, but he talked so quickly and indistinctly that at last I gave up trying and began to think of other things.

I was delighted that the worst part of the confession was over. I felt inclined to jump for joy. The rest was quite easy. I only had to finish the last half of the "confiteor," and I knew I shouldn't make a mistake in that.

When the priest had finished lecturing he said, "Say for your penance, my child, five Our Father's and five Hail Mary's, and may God's blessing be with you."

I thought it was a very easy penance for all the sins he thought I'd been committing; but I didn't say so. I just said, "Thank you, Father," and got up and came out of the confessional.

Having your sins forgiven makes you feel clean and fresh, as you do after a bath. When I had finished saying my penance I happened to glance up at the picture of St. Mary Magdalene, and I loved her for looking at me so gently. The chapel was pretty and peaceful in the soft light, and it seemed to me as though the Virgin Mary and St. Joseph and the Baby and all the other saints in the chapel were stretching their arms out to me, glad that I was happy. I felt I loved them too, I was ready to love everybody in the world, because I was so relieved that my first confession was over. And then I remembered that it was really God who had been so kind to me all the time, and that I was wicked and ungrateful not to love Him too. I began to love Him at once. I loved Him so much that I cried and hid my face on the top of the prie-Dieu. I was afraid lest I should make a noise, and I stuffed my handkerchief into my mouth and bit it to keep myself quiet. When I once loved God it was easy to be sorry for having offended Him, and I was. I thought I could never be wicked again, because He had been so merciful and because I need no longer dread my first confession drawing nearer and nearer. The more I loved Him the more I cried, till Reverend Mother came up and touched me on the shoulder and said, "Come, my child."

I wiped my eyes and followed her out of the chapel, and when we were outside she stopped and patted my head and said, "Good little penitent! I was praying all the time that you should be enabled to make a good confession. I can see that God has heard my prayer."

But it wasn't her prayers. It was because I had been so

wicked and God had forgiven me as soon as I asked and did not intend to punish me, and because my hateful first confession was over at last.

I hardly spoke to any one all the rest of that day because I felt so grave. But I was very happy.

Convent Life

I stayed for two years in the convent, and the longer I stayed the happier I was. I loved the nuns because they were kind and gentle, and however naughty we were they forgave us as soon as we asked them to and forgot our naughtiness. I liked the girls too, and they were fond of me. We thought it wrong to feel angry or unforgiving to anybody. When we quarrelled we made peace again as soon as possible, and if we could not do it ourselves, the nuns would help us. They told us we must always forgive any one who offended us because we wished God to forgive us. And we did. There were some Protestants among us, and we forgave them too, and tried not to think ourselves any better than they were.

The convent was divided into two parts. One part was called the "Middle School." That was for girls who were not the daughters of ladies and gentlemen as we were, but only the daughters of men and women. Their fathers were for the most part tradesmen or shopkeepers. They came and went at different doors. Their playground was at the side of ours, but there was a path with trees between us. We could see them and we knew them quite well by sight, but we were not supposed to, and if we met them in the street we never said, "How do you do?" but looked the other way as though we hadn't seen them. That was because they were not so well born as we were and didn't pay so much for their education. But we knew that they went to heaven just the same.

Soon after I was converted we had a new Reverend Mother. She was very old. Her face was yellow and wrinkled, but she was much kinder than the first one. She was always nodding her head and smiling, like the little china men and women who sit in the shop windows with their heads on balancing screws. When she was told of any of us being naughty she used to nod her head and smile and wrinkle up her eyes and say, "Oh, dear, dear! but I'm sure she will do better now."

And, of course, we said we would.

Every week, on Saturday morning, we assembled in the big hall and Reverend Mother and three of the nuns sat at a table at one end of it and gave out conduct tickets.

There were three kinds of conduct tickets. One was pale blue (the Blessed Virgin's colour) and marked "very good," another was red and marked "good," and a third was green and marked "indifferent." The nuns said that once there had been some yellow ones marked "bad," but they went out of print because they were never required.

Reverend Mother called out the names and smiled and held out the tickets, and each girl went up and took her own, and made a bow and came back again with a red face. When any of us got an "indifferent" Reverend Mother said, "It's the very last time I'm going to give you this, now, isn't it?"

And we always said, "Yes, Reverend Mother."

If we had said, "No, Reverend Mother," she would have been offended.

We had beautiful grounds at the back of the convent for recreation. There were a long shady garden and a tennis lawn and a big asphalt playground. We played cricket and tennis and rounders and "prisoners," and we were never allowed to sit down for one minute or to talk together in twos or threes. That was because, firstly, it was bad for our health, and secondly, because secret societies which are abominably wicked and plot against Church and State are always begun by people sitting and whispering together in twos and threes. So it's a really bad habit.

When we were at meals or needlework a nun sat at the head of the table and read to us. The nun who read most frequently was an Irish nun called Mother K. She was very clever and quite young. Her front teeth were prominent and her face was covered with freckles, and sometimes a little wisp of bright red hair used to peep out from under her coif. She was tall and stooped a little, and her green eyes had a kind, mild expression. When they looked at you they seemed to grow bright and affectionate at once. There was nothing interesting that she could not tell you everything about.

She read to us many very interesting books: adventures and novels (though she always left out the part in which the characters made love to one another. I knew because I'd read most of them before). She was supposed once a week to read to us from the lives of the saints, but we begged so hard to be let off that she very seldom did. It wasn't that we weren't interested in the saints, but the religious books sounded unreal after the others. We often coaxed her not to read at all but to let us ask her questions, and she would, and sat with her hands in her lap and her eyes shining and told us wonderfully interesting things—about the sea or the stars, foreign countries or anything we wished. We liked it much better than the reading.

Once a fortnight we each wrote an essay and stood up and read it aloud in class. The essays were generally successful. We wrote one on Shakespeare, and said that he was "*England's brightest star*," and another on Napoleon, and said that he was "*a terrible example to the grasping and ambitious*," and another on Cardinal Newman, and said that he was "*beloved by God, and therefore brought to light*," and so he was. We also wrote one on the "*Ideal Woman*," and said that she must be good-tempered and truthful, and fond of fair play and babies, and clean in her person, so as to give a good example to her husband and children. And the nun in charge said, must she not be modest and pious and intelligent, so as to bring up her children as good Catholics in the fear of God? We said we supposed so, but we had not thought to mention it. One girl said she must be obedient, and another shouted "Bosh!" so loudly that she made us all jump and got a bad mark for impoliteness.

After the essay on the "Ideal Woman" we wrote one on the "Ideal Man," and the nun was grieved and shocked because we nearly all paid more attention to his appearance and hair-dressing than to whether he was really to be trusted and had a nice character.

I said mine must be dark and clean-shaved with a square chin and a fearless eye. Most liked ideal men to be clean-shaved, but some liked wavy auburn hair and a drooping moustache, and some liked pointed beards, and one preferred a shaved head like a German officer. They all hated whiskers, and everybody wanted hair and beards to be carefully attended to and not ragged. One said that no man could look really like an aristocrat unless he used a little brilliantine. One said that no man must smell of scented soap, but others liked scented soap.

When the nun had listened to everything she said it

was very wrong of us to give a thought to anybody's personal appearance. What was important was that a man should be honourable and fearless and ready to die at the stake for the true religion. If God had not vouchsafed him the greatest blessing He can vouchsafe to any man—to be a priest and do His work in that way—then at least he should console himself by devoting the whole of his strength and wisdom to the establishment of love and justice and the maintenance of God's Church on earth.

Once a year we had a literary competition, when the girls from the four convents of the same order in London competed to write the best short story. The best story from each convent was sent to the central convent to be judged, and the story that was best of all was put into the library of the central convent.

We signed the stories with artificial names, and Reverend Mother read them aloud to the bigger girls and the principal nuns. They each voted for the story they liked best, and the story that got the most votes was considered the best story.

I was afraid my story would not be the best because most of the other girls lit candles to Our Lady or their favourite saints overnight and prayed for *inspiration*. But I did not; and that was really being guilty of the sin of presumption. But it was not really because I thought the Blessed Virgin could not have helped me. I was so excited about writing the story that I forgot about the candle.

As soon as Reverend Mother began to read the stories I felt sure mine would be the worst, because each one she read sounded more clever than the last. As she went on I was more and more sorry that I had not lit a candle.

Some of the stories were about virgins who had pined away, gnawed with despair, and died of disease in lonely towers rather than renounce the Catholic faith; and some about saintly hermits who had been roasted on hot cinders and scalped and suffocated and skinned alive, and yet persisted in proclaiming the true religion although the heathens and Protestants did all they could to stop them.

There was a realistic one about a shipwreck which ran something like this: "The wind moaned, the sea swelled, and the panting ship sank into the yawning gulf without a struggle, while women's hearts were wasting in the West."

That was the one I feared most. I thought it so very pathetic. There was another one about a bird that sat on a branch outside its nest, singing, singing, singing to its little ones full of joy, till a false, cold-hearted cat, that had always pretended to be friendly, came and ate up the little ones while their mother fell dead of anguish. That was very well written, but not so striking as the one about the shipwreck.

Then there was one about an urchin boy who died of hunger on a rich man's doorstep. But that was not convincing, because the rich man knew he was there all the time and could easily have fed him, but didn't. There were no proper explanations given.

My story was signed "Nero." It wasn't long, but it was very full of incident.

It was about an anarchist, who began life as a pageboy, but was lazy from the first. He would not stir a finger to help his mother keep his nine little brothers and sisters, but ate up all the scraps; and the older he got the more anarchist he became. As he grew up he joined all sorts of pernicious secret societies and signed treacherous proclamations in his own blood. He tried to make the soldiers and policemen defy the Pope and massacre the king and court, and when they refused he reviled them.

The reason of his wickedness was that he was really in the hands of the devil (I put that into the story to make it religious), and whenever he did anything particularly bad the devil appeared on his left-hand side and looked over his shoulder in scarlet and grinned and laughed, "ha-ha!" (not an honest, manly laugh, but an artful, mocking snigger), and his guardian angel appeared on his right hand in white muslin and wept to see the shocking way in which he was going on. But he didn't know they were there, and nothing stopped him.

He grew worse and worse. The story told many of the sinful things he did. One was that when the inhabitants of a burning house that had been set on fire by another anarchist put their heads out of the window and besought him to help them, he defied them and refused. He flung up his cloak over his left shoulder and tossed his head and said, "Burn, pernicious brood, a fitting holocaust to victorious anarchy!" and they did. (They were all aristocrats of the best sort.)

It took me some time to get the sentence about the holocaust into shape. Spelling didn't count in that competition or I should have put another one.

This anarchist went from bad to worse, but nothing he ever did succeeded. And when the other anarchists saw that he was unable to make the soldiers and policemen revolt and misbehave they scorned him and refused to be his friends. So he went on getting poorer and poorer and more and more lonely and sorrowful, and at last, when he had no more money and was thoroughly tired of being wicked, he met a Catholic priest who had also been an anarchist in his young days, but had been converted. Then the other anarchist was converted and became a priest too, and they died in one another's arms.

Some of the girls cried at the description of how they

died, and one of the nuns wiped her eyes. I didn't like the story much, but I thought the nuns might because of the conversion of the anarchists. And they did.

When the votes had been counted up, Reverend Mother smiled and said, "I congratulate 'Nero' on having written the best story, and I fully endorse the verdict of 'Nero's' companions."

Then everybody except myself began to clap, and my face grew red and they guessed who "Nero" was. They gathered round and began to congratulate me. It was not good for me, because it put me in danger of the sins of *pride* and *arrogance*, but I offered up three morning masses a week for the gift of *humility*, and after a long time it helped and I forgot about the competition.

It was a good thing, because there were many other things for which I wished to offer morning mass. I needed so many gifts to keep my soul in good condition. One must be so careful.

I never missed the early mass, though I was often rather sleepy. The candles were alight on the altar; the boy who served was clean—he had not had time to get soiled—and except for yawning he behaved beautifully. When he rang the little bells at the offertory they sounded like silver chimes.

I liked best when Father W. said mass. Father A. made one feel uneasy. He prayed so fervently and bowed so low, and looked so grave and ghostly, that he seemed not to belong to the world at all. He glided noiselessly about, and his face was white and intent, as though he were seeing God and listening to Him. There were so many shadows on it that when he turned, facing us, he was like a picture of Death, in long robes and with a frightful grinning skull for a head. When he spread out his hands they looked as bony and brittle as chickens' claws.

When it was Father G.'s turn (the priest I had made my first confession to), he waddled about with his small eyes turned up to heaven and his fat cheeks shaking like jellies. He was protrudant in front and gabbled off the mass as quickly as though he had not a moment to waste and was anxious to get home to breakfast.

But Father W. looked beautiful and saintly in his golden robes. He wore his spectacles right on the end of his nose, and he was so stiff that it was difficult for him to get up and down the altar steps. When the boy held up the gospel for him to read he clasped his hands and looked down his nose through his spectacles and spoke rather indistinctly because he had lost some of his teeth. But it was in Latin and we should not have understood in any case, so it did not matter. The candle-light shone in his white hair and made a golden mist round his head, and when he turned round and stretched out his arms to us to say the "Pax Vobiscum," he looked full of love and very old and humble.

I liked evening benediction too, when the organ

played and the choir sang. Then I loved God most of all. The altar was brilliant with flowers and candles, and the golden spikes round the monstrance shone like sun rays. People from outside came to benediction, so that the chapel was often full, and there was a very solemn, thrilling feeling in it. At times I used to cry when the litany was sung, and other girls did also. It was because the music was so grave and gentle and the lights so bright and the shadows so quiet. The soprano solo was sung by Mother R., a German nun with a peculiarly long nose, round bright eyes, and a stiff way of holding her head. She was so agitated when she sang that her cheeks and part of her nose grew red and her eyes filled with tears. She had a sweet, sharp voice like a bird's, and it seemed to dart about the chapel, in and out the shadows and up into the roof. The contralto solo was sung by a girl called M. H., a Protestant. She had a deep rich voice, like black rolls of velvet, and many people cried during the litany when she came to, "Lamb of God, which takest away the sins of the world."

That is the most solemn part of the litany. The chapel is always very still while it is being sung. People hold their breath and bow their heads. M.'s voice trembled when she sang it, as though she were afraid of something.

When her father heard that she sang in the chapel he was angry because she was a Protestant. He forbade her to sing any more and she cried herself into a fever. Her father came to take her away, and said that he would have her voice trained that she might sing at concerts, but she did not wish to. It was the "Lamb of God" in the litany that she liked singing, with the lights and flowers on the altar and the people kneeling, listening to her. Then her father gave way and allowed her to sing again, and next day when she came out of the chapel she fell on her knees at Reverend Mother's feet in the corridor outside, and said, "I want to be a Catholic! I want to be a nun!"

And Reverend Mother said, "You cannot go against your father's wishes."

M. fell into hysterics and the doctor was sent for. The same night her father came and took her home. But she ran away from home back to the convent and declared she would kill herself if she was taken away again. So she was allowed to stay and she sang in the chapel more and more beautifully. Whenever she had sung she used to cry because she was forbidden to be a Catholic.

There was another girl in the convent who wished to be a nun but was not able to. She thought the world outside so wicked that she could be safe only in a convent. She was afraid even of going for a walk. She was very small and weak with a tiny pointed face like that of a mouse and little round green eyes. She was old enough to be a nun, but she could not pass the examinations, and she was too delicate to stand the hard life and the fasting. But she always wore a black dress and shaved her head so as to look as much like a nun as possible. She did everything she could to grow cleverer and stronger. She passed hours together kneeling by the altar rails in the chapel praying for brains and strength, and often fainted before she could be made to come away. She would jump up every now and then to light a fresh candle. She spent all her spare money on candles, but it did not seem to be of any use. She remained just as unintelligent and weak. She constantly went to the doctor to see if there was any hope, and came back with her eyes red from crying because he said she was not stronger. Every time she heard she had failed in an examination she would lie ill in bed for a whole day crying. The nuns used to tell her that it was evidently not God's will that she should be a nun, and that she must try to serve Him in some other way; but nothing could comfort her. She talked of nothing but becoming a nun, and asked us a hundred times a day whether we thought she would ever be one. If we said yes, she would throw her arms round us and kiss us, and if we said no, she would cry. At last she grew weaker and weaker and died, partly, it was said, of fretting.

Nuns lead hard lives and have tiny bedrooms with no furniture but a crucifix, a little mat near the bed and a chair and washstand. They are not allowed to let their hair grow long or to look in the glass, and they get up very early in the morning in the dark to pray while other people are still warm in bed. Prayers must be said, and if ordinary people are too lazy to get up and do it religious people have to bear the consequences.

Nuns fast very often and take nothing but bread and water, and they refuse especially dainty food in case they should fall into the sin of *greed*. Whatever they least like to do they must do as often as possible in order to *mortify the flesh*; because the catechism teaches us that human nature is so bad that whatever we feel inclined to do is nearly certain to be wrong, and in the end will lead us to hell.

Nuns are not allowed to grow very much attached to people because God does not like it and is afraid they might get to love somebody better than Him. If a nun shows much affection for the girls or is a favourite with them she usually disappears and is sent away to another convent.

Nuns are not allowed to fall into a temper, raise their voices in anger, or slap one another as ordinary people do, and so their calling is not popular. The girls in the convent did not like to sit on a chair where a nun had been sitting or kneel in a place in the chapel where a nun had been kneeling for fear of "*catching a vocation*," as though it were measles. Most nuns are contented with their lives. Some make rope ladders out of sheets and let themselves down through the window and run away; but most of them don't. Mother W., who taught us catechism, was a merry nun. One day when the lesson was upon "Holy Orders," she said that people imagined that nuns were women who had had some disappointment in love and went into the convent to cure their sorrow, which was nonsense. She had become a nun because she liked the life and thought it was the proper way of serving God. She said that nuns were for the greater part like her.

I had no wish to become a nun. I was not good enough, and the older I got the worse I became. I fought against all sorts of sins and vices, but it was no good. My soul grew blacker and blacker; I could feel it doing it. I was more and more filled with irreverent curiosity, and I found it more and more difficult to believe without asking questions. If you cannot believe without asking questions it means you lack faith, and if you lack faith you cannot be a proper child of God. But I could not help asking questions. When I did so during "religious instruction," the nuns told me not to interrupt but to ask questions privately, and when I did that they usually said that God does not really mean us to understand much down here, but that everything would be properly explained after the last day. I was so impatient that I felt I could not wait until the last day, which was being guilty of the sin of *audacity*. Even when I gave up asking questions I secretly wondered, and that is nearly as bad, and comes from want of *reverence*.

A very pious and learned priest called Monsignor C. R. used to come to the convent about once a month to give us special religious instruction, and then we put our gloves on to show respect and sat in rows in the big hall to listen to him.

He was so fat that he bulged out of his armchair on all sides. Wherever there was an opening in the chair a piece of him protruded. His nose was so long and heavy that it hung down over his upper lip, and his upper lip was so long and heavy that it hung down over his lower lip. His cheeks were fat and hung down too, and so did his double chin.

He used to sit in the chair with his legs apart and pant, and try to fold his hands together over his stomach, but it was so big that he could hardly do so. He gasped and wheezed between each sentence, so that it took him a long time to say the simplest thing, and we dared not move or cease looking interested.

He used to question us about what we should answer if heretics made mocking or unfriendly inquiries about our religion. Every time he asked a question he raised his eyebrows as high as they could go, opening his smeary little eyes; and as soon as somebody began to answer he dropped them again with a sort of snap, and frowned and thrust his lips out as much as to say, "I know you're going to make a mistake."

I used to stare at his big nose and thick lips and fishy eyes, and wonder what they would look like if I made a blasphemous reply to one of his questions. I longed so much to do so that I was afraid I might one day forget myself.

Once he asked us, "What would you answer if a Protestant were to say to you: 'Why do you reverence the personal relics of the saints?'"

A blasphemous reply came into my head in a moment. It was: "Because hair and teeth will always fetch their price."

My grandfather's cook had once said that when talking of her own false set. I begged God's forgiveness at once. But blasphemous answers to all such questions instantly occurred to me. I could not prevent it, so that I was obliged to keep begging forgiveness at the time.

Argumentativeness was another of my more serious sins. Once at evening recreation when it was wet and we stayed indoors and had general conversation with Mother W. I began an argument about anarchists. I insisted that they were not really so bad as people thought them. I said that once I had lived with anarchists and that they were very talented people who wrote plays and talked French better than many people who were not anarchists.

Mother W. was shocked and said I did not know what I was saying. She reminded me that I had pointed out in my own story how terribly wicked it was to be an anarchist, and I answered that my anarchist was only so wicked because he was in the hands of the devil who had been invented by religious people.

Mother W. was still more shocked and her face grew red, but the other girls were interested. And when I saw that I became still more audacious. Mother W. said that anarchists wished to destroy the Church, and threw bombs at rich people in order to steal their money. I replied that anarchists wrote splendid leading articles and made important speeches and were extremely particular whom they made friends with. She said that she had never heard such things said as I was then saying, and I said that if she went to Hyde Park on a Sunday she would hear many clever and noble people saying much worse, and that I had often been there and asked them for their autographs.

Then Mother W. was so angry that she could not sit down any longer. She stood up and said that anarchy was a dreadful evil, condemned by the Church, and that to encourage it and believe in it was to be in a state of mortal sin. I was angry too, and blasphemous. I said that being an anarchist was much healthier and more interesting than being religious, and that as soon as I had finished my education I should at once become an anarchist again.

The girls were still more interested. They stared and listened in perfect silence.

Mother W. by then could hardly speak. She walked to the door and opened it, and motioned to me to go out. When I reached the door she told me to go to my room and think how wrong I had been. She said she would speak to Reverend Mother. The girls had begun whispering together.

I went out and up to my room. I opened the window and leant my elbows on the sill, although it was raining, and looked out into the quadrangle. There was nobody there, but the plants were all bright green and dripping with rain.

I tried to make an "act of contrition," but my heart was hard and I was unable to do so. I gave myself to wicked rebellious feelings. I was angry because Mother W. insisted that all anarchists were wicked when I knew they were not. I remembered how happy I had been when I was an anarchist, and how interesting it was making propaganda in the Park and instructing policemen. I thought about my grandfather and wished I could see him. I knew he would have listened to everything and have tried to explain, instead of being so positive and obstinate as Mother W.

I felt utterly desolate and began to cry; but just then a lay sister came in with my supper on a tray, so I pretended to be making signs to some one in the quadrangle, and laughed, so that she should not know I had been crying and tell the other nuns.

It was the lay sister who came to brush my hair in the morning. I loved her because she was so pretty and gentle. She had a soft, bright face like a flower, and blue eyes and little pearly teeth. When she brushed my hair her hands were so light and tender that I hardly felt them, and she never tugged at the tangles.

She did not smile now as she generally did, but looked serious and put my supper on the table and told me Reverend Mother had said that I was not to come down again that night. I pretended not to care; but I did. I felt I could not bear to be lonely like that all the evening. I longed to take hold of her rosary and tell her I knew that I was wicked and that I'd try to be better, and ask her not to look so grave as if she did not like me. But I was too proud, and she went out of the room without speaking, and I began to cry again.

I didn't eat my supper (I was exceedingly hungry, but I was too proud), and I went to bed feeling very miserable. It was the first time in my life that I had gone to bed knowing that some one was angry with me.

❧❧❧

I did not go to mass next morning. The lay sister brought my breakfast into my room and told me to wait there. At first I thought I should be left alone again all day, but when mass was finished Reverend Mother sent for me.

She was waiting for me in the corridor outside the chapel with her eyes screwed up and her hands folded in her sleeves. When she saw me she smiled and nodded her head as usual and said to me, "We are going for a little walk in the garden."

And we did. We walked side by side down the gravel path between the trees. Reverend Mother's head kept on nodding a little as she walked and her hands were still folded in her sleeves. I knew that the girls at morning preparation in the big schoolroom could see us walking together, and it made me feel important. It was only when a girl had done something very bad that Reverend Mother took her walking in the garden.

She said that Mother Woodward had told her the night before how strangely I had talked at evening recreation. She could hardly believe that one of her girls could have talked like that. If I had been a wild girl or a heathen who had never known the blessing of having been admitted to the true religion she would have understood it, but as it was there was no excuse. She said, "I am sure you did not understand the seriousness of what you said."

I said, no, I didn't think it was so serious, and that lots of people said the same as I had said.

Reverend Mother said, not pious Catholics, and that when people talked like that it was only because they had not had the advantages of education and religious instruction and so had never had a chance to learn the truth. She said that very often irreligious words lightly spoken were the cause of great spiritual trials and temptations, and that, by speaking carelessly as I had done, I might have been exposing my companions to spiritual danger. Then she said, "I am sure you will be more careful in the future, will you not?"

And I said, "Yes, Reverend Mother."

Then she smiled and stopped, and turned to look at me and said, "It's getting time for you to make your first communion."

Her face looked very kind and glad when she said that, as if she thought it ought to make me happy. I looked down on the ground and said, "Yes, Reverend Mother."

And when I looked up she was still standing looking at me, and smiling and nodding her head. Then she patted me on the shoulder and told me to run into the house and make my peace with Mother W., and I said, "Thank you, Reverend Mother" (we had to), and walked up the path. I could see the girls in the big classroom bobbing up and down in their seats to watch me, and when I came near enough some of them waved their hands to me. But I took no notice. I went to look for Mother W.

She was watering the plants in the quadrangle. She had her back to me and didn't see me, and I went up and stood beside her and said, "Please forgive me, Mother, for arguing about anarchists, and please do not be angry with me."

She was very kind. She forgave me at once (nuns always do) and said, "Well, my child, then let us forget all about it."

Then she told me to remember that the nuns were fond of me and thought I did my lessons well, and looked to me to give a good example to the smaller girls now that I was growing big, and that it would always pain them if they thought they could not trust me. She said it showed want of respect to God and to the nuns to joke about things that were really very serious.

But I had not been joking.

When I went into the big classroom the girls turned round and stared at me as if I was something very interesting, and when the bell rang for classes they came round to me to ask where I had been the night before, and what Reverend Mother had been saying to me. But I did not answer. When the day girls came the others told them what had happened during evening recreation, and for a long time afterwards they used to ask me about my life among anarchists, and what they were like. But I did not tell them, because I did not want to grieve the nuns when they had been so kind to me.

❧❧❧

Three of us made our first communion together during mass in the chapel one morning about two months after I had spoken about anarchists and been forgiven.

We had special instruction from a priest for about a month beforehand in order to make us really fit for the blessing we were about to receive. In the intervals between the instruction we were allowed special time in the chapel for meditation.

The priest said that when our Lord at the Last Supper pronounced the words, "This is My body. This is My blood," over some bread and wine, He really meant it, and that ever since then Catholic priests had been able to change bread and wine into the body and blood of Christ by the power of God when they said the same words at mass. What we swallow when we go to communion is not really flour made up into a wafer (as we should think it was if we had not been told), but it is the true flesh of Christ, and as it is so merciful and gracious of Christ to come down on to the altar and turn into bread and wine for our benefit, we must be in a special state of grace to receive Him. He told us other things besides, but that was what mattered most.

I did not feel glad I was going to make my first communion. I was afraid I should not make a good one, and that when the priest put the sacred host on the tip of my tongue I should not be able to believe it was our Lord Himself. It did not seem natural. And if the sacred host really was our Lord Himself, it did not seem the proper thing to do with it. I did not believe I ought to swallow it, but the priest said I ought. Swallowing a person is not the proper way to show respect even if you are in the highest state of grace. But the priest said it was quite right and that no mistake had been made.

Even then I did not feel confident about it; but that was because I was lacking in faith and had not been brought up in the true religion from a baby as the others had. They did not seem to think there was anything peculiar about it. They thought, in fact, that it was wrong to make conjectures about anything one ought to believe; that was because they had plenty of faith. I longed to argue about it, but I did not because it would have grieved the nuns and put my companions into spiritual danger.

I used to stare at the sacred host during mass and benediction, and wonder if it could be the living body of our Lord, and if it was, how the priest dared to fix it into the monstrance and take it out again as he did in benediction, and carry it about and lift it over his head and put it back into the chalice when he had done with it, and shut it up in the tabernacle after mass and go away to breakfast as if nothing had happened. It seemed to me that if the priest really believed the host was our Lord alive upon the altar he would be almost afraid to touch it, and ready to die with joy at being allowed to approach anything so sweet and sacred, instead of trotting about with it and gabbling over it hastily as Father G. did when he said mass. I used to watch Father G. and wonder if he really cared in the least for what he was doing.

Once when I had stayed on in the chapel after mass for meditation I heard some one snoring in the sacristy. The door was open, and it could be heard quite plainly all over the chapel. It was the priest who had just been saying mass. He had come from a long distance to do it and had had to get up earlier than usual. He was very tired and had fallen asleep.

It made me cry to think that he could be so cold and thoughtless as to lie there snoring with our Lord in the tabernacle listening to him. I thought Christ must be grieved to think that people could be near Him and forget Him. They should be kneeling and praying in the chapel day and night if they really believed that He is in the tabernacle waiting for them. The more I thought about it the more I cried, and when I came out of the chapel my eyes were red and the nuns asked me what was the matter. But I was obstinate and would not tell them.

When the morning for our first communion came we were dressed in white muslin and white lace veils that fell to the bottom of our dresses. (I wore the same dress I was baptised in, but it had to be let down all round.) We each carried a clean handkerchief, a rosary and prayer-book in our hands to show respect, and when all the nuns and children and visitors were in their places we walked in procession up the chapel and knelt down in three prie-Dieu at the top near the altar rails. I suppose we looked very impressive, because everybody was so quiet when we came in.

I felt extremely nervous. Father W. was saying mass, and as the time drew near for us to rise and kneel at the altar to take communion I felt more and more so.

At last the moment came. Reverend Mother appeared from somewhere and stood beside us and gave us the signal to rise and we did so. I followed the other two to the foot of the altar, and we knelt there in a row and waited for the priest to bring the host to us.

He turned round and began to move with the chalice towards us. I longed for him to stop. I felt I could not remain there and let him put the host upon my tongue. I should have liked to get up and run out of the chapel, but I dared not.

I was the last to receive communion. I could see sideways how the other two clasped their hands and bowed their heads down on the altar rails when they had taken the host as they had been taught to do. They did it perfectly, without the slightest hesitation, but when my turn came I felt I could hardly breathe because my heart was thumping so. I imagined that when the priest put the host on my tongue it would suddenly grow heavy and jerk my head down and make me knock my chin against the altar rails. When he did put it there I felt nothing at all but something light and tasteless on my tongue. But I was so frightened that there seemed to be a mist before my eyes and a buzzing in my ears, and the priest appeared to fade away through the mist and up the altar steps again like a spirit. I forgot what I had to do. I did not clasp my hands and bow my head in the right manner, and I did not get up and follow the others back to the prie-Dieu as we had rehearsed it. I knelt there till a nun came and touched me on the shoulder. When I got up the mist in front of my eyes was so thick and the buzzing in my ears so loud that I did not know which way to go, and the nun led me back to the prie-Dieu like a blind girl. But when I knelt down my eyes grew suddenly clear again, the noise in my head ceased, and everything seemed strangely quiet. I could feel the host on the middle of my tongue, and for a moment I forgot how it had come there and what I ought to do with it. Then I remembered that I had made my first communion, that Christ was with me, and that I ought to welcome Him. But I did not feel as though the little lump of melting wafer could be Christ. Then I remembered that supposing it really were Christ it might slip down my throat without my having said a word to Him, and the chance would be gone. The thought made me so nervous that I suddenly felt a stiffening in my throat and my jaws seemed tightly fixed and as rigid as iron. I thought I was about to choke. I clutched the prie-Dieu, and my forehead grew wet with perspiration. When I found that nothing happened and that there was no danger of my choking if I kept my tongue still and let the host lie quietly on it, I recovered a little and tried to say the Act of Adoration I had learnt by heart. But I could not remember it. The host was slipping right to the back of my tongue, and all of a sudden I clutched at the prie-Dieu again with my heart beating wildly and gave a strangled gulp and the host slipped down my throat. I was glad that it had gone down safely and that I had not choked or screamed. As it went it left a flavour in my mouth like that of the wafers that are eaten with ices, and when I tasted that I suddenly felt sure it was not Christ. I felt as certain as if God Himself had bent down and whispered it to me. I seemed to wake suddenly out of a dream. I was not frightened any longer. I was surprised that I had been so frightened. I looked round me and the chapel had grown somehow different. It no longer seemed holy and mysterious. The priest seemed to be just an ordinary man reading out of ordinary books and moving ordinary things about the altar. It seemed strange for him to be doing it all so solemnly with so much ceremony.

The altar seemed like an ordinary table and the candles like ordinary candles with nothing sacred about them. The statues of the Virgin and St. Joseph seemed to have turned into great staring dolls. I suddenly felt sure that it was all a mistake to think there was anything mysterious about the priest and the things he did at mass. I longed to speak to somebody of this feeling, to see if they could understand it too. I could not imagine why I had never noticed it before. I knelt there and looked at the priest without attempting to pray, and when the time came for us to rise and leave the chapel I was not nervous. I got up and walked down the aisle looking about me and swinging my arms, instead of casting down my eyes and clasping the prayer-book in my hands with the rosary hanging down as I ought to have done. I did not feel at all as if anything unusual had been happening to me, and when the people came to congratulate us I felt as if they were making an absurd fuss about nothing. I felt inclined to say to them, "You are making a mistake. It is not Christ at all. Going to communion is not really wonderful."

But I said nothing. I hardly spoke all day. I felt as if I had discovered some great truth that I alone knew and that other people would not be capable of understanding if I told them.

I woke up in the night and thought about it again, and it seemed strange to be free not to believe without trying to force oneself to do so. It was a great relief—as though a heavy weight had fallen from my shoulders.

Next day, when I was going from one classroom to another, I met Reverend Mother and several of the other nuns walking down the corridor. Reverend Mother was walking in the middle, because she was the most important, and there were two or three nuns on either side of her. Whenever she spoke they bent their heads towards her to show respect and made no interruption.

I tried to slip into a classroom, but Reverend Mother smiled and beckoned to me and I went up to them. But I did not stand in the middle of the corridor. I squeezed up to the wall and pressed my back against it. I felt safer like that and not so shy.

The nuns stopped and stood round me in a circle, and Reverend Mother said, "Well, my little first communicant, don't you feel very happy at the blessing our dear Lord has conferred upon you?"

I looked down on the ground and pressed harder against the wall and made no answer. I was not frightened. Even the nuns seemed ordinary and not solemn and mysterious as they had seemed before I gave up making myself believe things. I glanced up for a moment at the white parts of their dresses that had always semed so pure and stately, and I thought to myself that they were only made of the same stuff as collars and cuffs, but in a different shape, and that their veils and robes were of common black material that any one could make a dress of. It seemed to me most strange to have such thoughts and not to correct them a moment later. I was glad there was no need to.

It was rude of me not to answer, and Reverend Mother thought I was shy. She said again, "Did it not make a most blessed and wonderful impression on your soul when our Lord came to visit you in person?"

At first I thought I would not reply, but then I was seized with a wicked curiosity to see what the nuns would look like if I said something blasphemous. I was standing on one foot with the other bent back on to the hot-water pipes behind me. I changed on to the other foot and backed against the wall again and looked down on the ground and said, "Not very much."

But the next minute I peeped up again because I wanted so intensely to see what effect my words would have.

It seemed as if each of them moved all over with surprise, and they opened their eyes wider and looked at me as if they could not take their eyes from my face.

And Reverend Mother said, "But, my child, did you not feel the inestimable blessing our Lord conferred upon you when He deigned in person to enter into your body?"

I changed on to the other foot again and looked terribly guilty and heretical, but I said again, "Not very much."

Then they seemed to grow so stiff with horror that I was almost afraid. I felt as if we had all been standing there for hours and no one spoke.

Then Reverend Mother said, "But, my child, do you not believe in the Blessed Sacrament?"

I felt my face growing redder and redder, and I wriggled against the wall and then stood on one foot again and looked down on the ground and said, "Not very much."

I could *feel* them grow still more petrified. I was still so full of impious curiosity that I could not help peeping up again to see what they looked like. They were still staring as before. Not one of them had moved.

Then Reverend Mother said, "I must see to this. I must speak to her," and she came out from the rest and put her hand on my shoulder, and the other nuns turned and went away without speaking. They looked like long, black shadows floating down the corridor, not one of them turning their heads or speaking to the others, and their footsteps were inaudible.

Reverend Mother kept her hand on my shoulder and took me into one of the classrooms. She shut the door behind us and then turned round to me and said, "What was the meaning of your words to me just now?"

I said, "Which words?"

And Reverend Mother said, "Is it possible that you don't believe the Blessed Sacrament to be the body and blood of our Lord? Did you not believe that our blessed Lord Himself had come to you when you made your first communion?"

I said, "At first I did a little; then I didn't."

Reverend Mother was so shocked that she could not speak for a moment. Then she said, "But what has come over you? What has caused you to lose your faith in such a terrible manner?"

I said, "Because the priest carries it about so much."

Reverend Mother asked, "Carries what about?"

And I said, "The sacred host. He could not do it if it were our Lord."

And she said, "But don't you know that the catechism tells us that it is done by the power of God, to Whom nothing is impossible or difficult?"

I was nervous no longer. I felt I was growing audacious.

I said, "God would not want to."

And she asked, "Would not want to what?"

I said, "To change our Lord into bread and wine and let Him be shut up in the tabernacle."

Reverend Mother was still more shocked, and I went on arguing. I said if it was true about the Blessed Sacrament the priest would not dare to snore so that our Lord could hear him, and the sacristan would not dust the tabernacle with a feather brush as though it were furniture.

Reverend Mother asked me what I meant about the priest's snoring, and I told her, and I said that the sacristan did not make nearly such a deep bow in front of the tabernacle when the chapel was empty as when there were people watching him. He made a careless little bob and went by. I had noticed that too, when I was meditating in the chapel.

Reverend Mother stared at me again for a moment, speechlessly, and then she said that in her whole life she had never been so surprised and horrified. She said she must have time to consider, and ask a priest's advice before she could decide what to say, or what to do with me.

She told me to go away, and as I was going she asked me if I had spoken to any of my companions in that manner. I said I had not, and she made me give her my word of honour not to do so. I gave it, but I noticed that, after that, during all the recreations a nun kept me by her side and would not let me mix with the other girls. That was because the nun was afraid I should forget my promise and put my companions into spiritual danger.

Next morning I was sent for into Reverend Mother's

room. Reverend Mother and the Mother Prefect were there together.

Reverend Mother said that after considering the matter for some time, she and the other nuns had made up their minds that it would be better for me to leave the convent at the end of the term. They did not wish to expel me, because that would put a slur on my character which I had done nothing to deserve. She said I was a good, industrious girl, but that they thought it would be better for me not to mingle with the other girls under their charge, because I had taken to such strange ways of thinking and speaking. Did I understand? And I said, "Yes, Reverend Mother."

And she said they would write to my relations and recommend them to send me to a certain convent in Germany.

Then she said, quite kindly, with no sign of anger, "The discipline in that convent is good, and perhaps they will do better for you there than we have been able to do, though believe me, my child, we have always tried to do our best."

She reminded me again that I had promised not to speak about the matter to the other girls, and I did not, and no one knew why I was going to leave.

When the time came I was extremely sorry to go, and the nuns said it grieved them to lose me. But they were quite sure that I should regain my religion in the German convent, and that it would be better for me in the end.

So I left, and went to Germany, and never saw the convent or the nuns again. But I often thought about them, and I shall always be grateful to them for having been so kind to me.

❖

CHAPTER FOUR

I Go to Germany

I went to Germany at the end of July, in order to spend some time with a German lady, Frau G., before the beginning of the term in the German convent. Frau G. lived in a little town on the banks of the Rhine, and I was taken there by a young English lady who was going to be a governess near the same place. She came to see me before starting, and we made friends. She looked so pretty and dainty that she reminded me of a china tea-cup in a best service. Her name was Miss H. She had blue eyes that curved up a little at the corners. Her lips curved upwards too, and when she smiled you could see a dimple in each cheek where it began to turn pink. When we started on the journey she wore a tiny black hat to show how golden her hair was, and some clean, frilly lace round her neck as white as snow. I thought her so pretty that I sat opposite her in the train and stared at her all the time, and a melancholy-looking German gentleman who got into the same carriage seemed to fall in love with her and stared too.

She did not mind my staring, but she disliked the German gentleman because he seemed so sentimental. He had a fat red face, and dull blue eyes, and a very sweet smile, and his hair-dressing was complicated. His head was shaved and covered with a stiff yellow down, and he had a little spiky moustache that stood out on both sides as stiffly and sharply as two darning needles.

Miss H. held up a newspaper in front of her face to hide it from him, and if she lowered it even for a moment the German gentleman drooped all over and smiled a melting smile as though imploring her to love him.

When we left the train to go on board the ship he followed close behind, and when we had stowed away our things and taken our places on deck we found that he had got a seat next to us.

It was a cold, windy day, although it was summer, and when we started the ship began to rock. I had never been on a ship before, and Miss H. thought I might be nervous. She put her arm round me and kissed me. When I saw that we were moving further and further from the land I was startled, and then I longed to put my arms out and cling on to it. My throat began to ache and tears came into my eyes and hid the coast from me. I hid my face against Miss H. and cried. She leant over me and wiped my eyes and waved her handkerchief to England and said to me, "Look up and say good-bye to England bravely, and when we come back we shall find her faithfully waiting for us."

I raised my eyes, but the further we went the more my heart ached, and I looked back until I couldn't see a trace of England.

Presently it grew rougher and Miss H. wrapped a rug round me and told me not to be alarmed if she was ill. The gentleman in love got up and staggered from one pillar to another until he got downstairs.

Miss H. was glad that he was gone. She said, "What an odious man!"

But in a few minutes he was back again looking more tender than before. He stood near us, swaying and clutching at a railing with one hand, and he gave us a little bow with his head and began to talk. He could be silent no longer. He said, in German, "Will the gracious Miss permit me to give her some advice?"

We couldn't help staring at him and wondering what he was going to say, and he said, "Perhaps the gracious Miss is not aware that upon the ocean repleteness is ever advisable?"

At first we could not understand what he meant, but afterwards he explained and made it clear.

He said that he had been down below and eaten everything he could lay hands upon. He had even eaten pies and sandwiches that other people wanted to buy, and had drunk a great many glasses of beer. He was replete with things to eat and drink. He said that on a ship that was the best thing to do, because then if Nature made demands upon you it was not so difficult to comply.

He looked at Miss H. and smiled brightly, and bowed with his head again and said, "Jawohl!" (German).

But she stared the other way and would not take any interest.

Then he sat down on my side (there were some ropes on the other), and leant forward and looked at Miss H. round me and said, "Will the gracious Miss do me the honour to drink a glass of beer with me?"

Miss H. looked the other way and pretended not to understand. Then he leant forward again and said, coaxingly, "Drink then a glass of beer, Miss. Beer is, in such cases, an unspeakable consolation."

He looked full of affection, but Miss H. said stiffly, "No, thank you."

But he could not bear to be so coldly repulsed; he longed to do something to show his love. He said, "Eat then something, Miss. The pork pies are remarkable. With a pork pie in the stomach can one peacefully travel further."

But she said again, in an icy manner (she was beginning to feel sea-sick), "No, thank you."

And he said, "Gott!" ("God!").

He looked very sad. He ought, of course, to have behaved in a more romantic manner, being in love. But he probably did not know.

Miss H. was very ill, and we were extremely glad to get off the ship into the train. We went into a carriage marked "Damen," where no gentleman would ever dare to follow. The gentleman in love would have been glad to, but he knew it was impossible, so he put his portmanteau down in the corridor outside our window and stood like a statue staring in. Miss H. felt so ill that she was quite indifferent. She leant back in a corner with her smelling-salts to her nose and paid no attention. After a little while she went to sleep and I grew tired of sitting by myself, so I got up and slipped into the corridor past the German gentleman and looked out of one of the windows. But he followed me and began to talk. He said, sadly, in English, "English girls iss pretty, but, my Gott, how colt! One tries one's best, but cannot please them."

I said nothing and the German gentleman grew more excited, and said, "It iss goot ven ze man shall try to please ze voman and she iss pleased, but it iss not goot ven ze man shall try to please ze voman and she iss not pleased."

Then he frowned and went into a carriage and sat down in a corner and folded his arms, and left his portmanteau in the corridor where people tumbled over it. I think he forgot it because he was so grieved that Miss H. had not returned his affection.

I thought Germany a very pretty country. The grass and trees and hedges were thick and green and tidy. They looked expensive, somehow, as if a lot of money had been spent upon them. The cottages and farmhouses had a bright and comfortable appearance, and there were trees weighed down with apples standing along the roadsides. Sometimes we passed a little girl walking along a road in a clean black and white checked dress, with yellow hair hanging in a pigtail tied with a ribbon at the end. When she heard the train coming she would turn and wave her hand and smile, and I thought I should like to wear my hair in a pigtail instead of loose upon my shoulders. Every now and then at a crossing a tidy woman stood near the rails in a checked apron waving a flag. Once we passed a fox standing alone in the middle of a field with his head turned back over his shoulder to listen to the train. Sometimes I saw oxen pulling carts. The men in the carts had big, peaceful faces, and the oxen were fat and neat and looked expensive too, like the grass and trees and hedges. It all seemed like a painted toy that I should have liked to play with.

In the afternoon we arrived at K., a large, busy town. The streets seemed cleaner and the wheels smoother than in London. We were to pass the night there, before taking another train to B.

In K. everybody's hair is extremely tidy, and their boots are big and nicely blacked. Most people have round faces and straight backs and staring eyes. The gentlemen have beautifully brushed coats and keep on bowing and taking their hats off to the ladies, and the ladies hold their heads stiff and look hostile at the gentlemen.

We were met at the station by a German gentleman, the uncle of one of Miss H.'s pupils. He was a little, fat, elderly gentleman, with a spiky moustache, and round black eyes with a network of wrinkles at the corners and no whites to be seen. He had a big cigar in his mouth and wore a nicely-kept top hat a little on one side, and a very thick coat with a big velvet collar that reached half-way up the back of his head.

His name was Baron von Something (I did not catch his right name). He was evidently proud because he was so important. When he told the porters what to do with our luggage they bowed up and down and said, "Ja, Herr Baron" ("Yes, Mr. Baron") and, "Nein, Herr Baron" ("No, Mr. Baron"), and when he walked he wagged his coat tails from side to side, and if anybody got into his way he waved them out of it with his stick.

When we were outside the station he told us that he had two wonderfully beautiful houses in a wonderfully beautiful street, but he couldn't take us to them because his wife had quarrelled with him and forbidden it. He could not bring his carriage either, because his mother-in-law had quarrelled with him too and forbidden that. So we got into a hired carriage and drove about, as he said to see the town, but he showed us nothing but restaurants. He was very interested in restaurants, and whenever we passed a specially big one he made the carriage stop and stared at it and said was there anything in London to equal that? He told the coachman to drive some way out of the town so that we might see the restaurant he liked best of all. When we came to it we got out of the carriage and walked down a long hall with marble columns on each side, and waiters with napkins kept bowing up and down and saying, "Tag, Herr Baron" ("Good-day, Mr. Baron").

Then we came to an open-air place like a circus, with little chairs and tables stretching in circles down a slope until they came to a bandstand in the middle. It looked something like a picture of the amphitheatre in Rome.

The Baron admired this very much. He stood staring at it for a long time, until we were so tired that we sat down near one of the little tables to wait for him. He went on staring with his hat off as though he were in church. At last he sighed, put his hat on and said, "Da kann ein Mensch sich aber glücklich fühlen" ("There can a man feel himself happy").

Then he told us that one could sit at the little tables till late into the night, and order beer or chocolate or anything one had a fancy for. He said there was nothing one could mention or imagine that the restaurant could not provide, and that there was no restaurant in the civilised world to be compared to it.

For some time after we got back into the carriage he said nothing. He seemed dreadfully depressed. But then he recovered and told the cabman to drive us to another restaurant. It was in a big square with a very tall church in the middle. We went all over it. We looked into the big dining-rooms and the kitchens, and wine cellars and cupboards, and into some little private rooms, and the people in them were angry, but the Baron paid no attention. The waiters kept bowing up and down and saying, "Tag, Herr Baron," just as the other waiters had done. The Baron said that this restaurant was the second best in the civilised world.

Then we sat in a balcony overlooking the square and drank chocolate and ate tarts with piles of cream on them. The Baron was still very depressed. Suddenly he banged his fist on the table and pointed to the church in the middle of the square and said he would build a church four times as high if his mother-in-law would only die. He said, in German, "My wife I can manage, but the old cat—"

He said, would we believe that if his mother-in-law came down the street and saw him sitting in the balcony with two young ladies she would climb up and pull him off by the hair of his head.

I was very sorry for him. I understood now why he seemed so depressed. The more he talked about his "Schwiege-Mama" (mother-in-law) the angrier he grew, and all the while he continued eating tarts and cream and drinking cups of chocolate. He went on telling us about his mother-in-law.

He said that his wife was wonderfully beautiful, as stately as a queen and that she weighed twelve stone, but that his mother-in-law weighed more and thought she was more beautiful than the wife, and that whenever they went out the mother-in-law insisted on wearing jewellery that the wife ought to have worn, and then they quarrelled and both scolded him. The mother-in-law was continually going to the most expensive photographers and being photographed in the wife's jewellery, and when the wife saw the photographs she cried bitterly and quarrelled with her mother, and then they both scolded him. He said his mother-in-law ate more than any living woman and that nothing disagreed with her, but that she abused him on account of his appetite so that he never dared to eat enough in his own house. She forbade him to speak to other ladies for fear he should give them jewellery that otherwise he would have given to his wife, so that *she* could wear it, and when she went out in the street she wore such high heels to her shoes that little boys followed in a tail behind and made rude remarks. He said if it had not been for the restaurants where he could escape from them both and be at peace he would have hanged himself. When he had finished the tarts and chocolate he got up and paid the bill, and said he was going to take us to another restaurant on the other side of the square where he should have dinner. He said that sometimes he almost thought this was the best restaurant of all and that was why he had kept it to the last.

There were a number of fashionable people dining in the restaurant. They were even tidier than the people in the street, and many were very stout. They wore their napkins tied round their necks, and bent their heads down over their plates and ate quickly as though they were afraid the other people would finish first and snatch their food away from them.

The Baron was pleased to see so many people dining. He thought it proved that the restaurant was such a splendid one. He said, in German, "Hither can one peacefully bring a good appetite."

And he sat and watched them with his eyes shining. It was the first time he had looked cheerful. He said it had often comforted him in his darkest moments with his mother-in-law to think that there were places such as this where people could sit and enjoy good food with healthy appetites while everything was being so splendidly managed.

He ordered dinner for us, but said that he himself would take nothing, that he could hardly ever eat. I thought to myself that he couldn't very well be hungry yet, because he had only just finished the tarts and cream and chocolate; but I said nothing.

He asked me how much my grandfather had left, and I said I didn't know. He asked if he had kept an hotel, and I said no, he was an artist, and he shook his head as though he were sorry for him, and said, "Arme Mensch!" ("Poor Man!").

He went on watching the people eating until at last he could resist no longer, and he called the waiter and ordered dinner for himself, and tied his napkin round his neck, and ducked his head among the plates and glasses and began to eat as quickly as the others.

When we left the restaurant the lamps were lit, and the square looked very gay and pretty. The air was so clear that the lights shone like diamonds, and little electric trams were running backwards and forwards gleaming like streaks of fire. There was a band playing a waltz in the distance, and a great many people were strolling about enjoying the fine evening.

But we drove back to the hotel near the station and went to bed. I was glad to go, because I was so tired. I had never travelled so far before.

❧❧❧

Frau G.'s house had a long garden in front with an avenue of trees leading down to a big iron gate. We kissed one another good-bye at the gate. Miss H. said I should be braver if I went into the house alone, and that she was going to another house in B. and would come and see me very soon. I walked up the long avenue to the house. The door was opened by a very old servant in a white muslin apron with a piece of black lace on her head. Her face was pointed and very wrinkled. Her head shook slightly and her eyes were dim, and she screwed them up a little when she looked at me as if she could not see me very plainly. But she smiled kindly at me, and said, "Good-day, good-day, good-day, my little Fraulein," and hobbled across the hall in front of me to a room that looked like a drawing-room. The floor was polished, and there were green and red woollen mats spread about it, and chairs were standing tidily round the walls. At one end of the room was a sofa with a rug and a table in front of it and chairs set round. The sofa and chairs looked very stiff and hard. They were covered with pale green velvet

150

with a pattern upon it and lots of little brass-headed nails all round the edges.

On one wall was a big picture of the Virgin Mary ascending into heaven in blue and gold clothes, the same sort of clothes she had worn in the convent in London. The heaven was a very bright blue and there were a number of golden stars painted on it and all over the picture. There were other pictures too in broad gilt frames ornamented with leaves and bunches of grapes. Some were of young maidens in flowing scarves, with pink, surprised faces and staring eyes. They looked like relations of the Blessed Virgin. Others were of dining-room tables with bunches of bananas and rhubarb and poultry and other things to eat spread out upon them. All the pictures looked as if they were freshly painted every day.

I stood on one of the woollen mats (I was afraid to stand on the polished floor) and felt very sad and lonely. I wished I had never come to Germany. But suddenly I heard a sound of somebody breathing hard behind me, and I turned round and saw a fat little old lady in a black dress with a white lace cap on her head. She had a big forehead and a round face very fresh and rosy, and her eyes were blue and clear. This lady was Frau G. She looked at me intently for a time without speaking, and she kept on grunting and breathing hard. Then suddenly she smiled and her eyes shone and twinkled and made her face look kind and merry. She came a step nearer and took me in her arms and kissed me on the forehead and said, "Liebes Kind! Liebes Kind!" ("Dear child! Dear child!").

Her eyes beamed at me so brightly that I did not feel lonely any more.

We sat down opposite one another at the little table. Frau G. sat in the armchair and I sat in one of the little stiff chairs and we began to talk. At first she asked me how old I was, and many questions about myself and my relations and my life in my uncle's house. Then she asked me how I had displeased the nuns in London, and I told her. She said that I had been very wrong, that young people should not try to argue and decide things for themselves, because older people knew what was best for them. When people got older and wiser and sadder they had many thoughts that only the old and sad could understand, but that youth should be devoted to preparing for one's vocation in life, learning to be thrifty, and growing accustomed to discipline as the best preparation for future suffering and disappointment. Then she stopped and nodded her head and said, "So," but though she smiled her eyes had no twinkle in them now, but looked grave and sad. Then she said, in German, "And how much money did your grandpapa leave behind him when he died?"

I said I didn't know, and she asked, "How many houses did he have?"

I said one house (at a time), and she said, "And how many servants did he keep?"

I told her, and she said, "Did he not then save some money?"

I said I didn't know; I'd never asked any one; but I'd never seen him saving any, and she said, "God! How thriftless are the English."

Then she told me that in Germany everybody saved up money and spent as little as they could, and that was why they all got on so well. She said that she still had some of the savings of her youth to leave to her nephews and nieces and god-children, and that she made her own woollen mats and bed linen and embroidered the table covers and curtains to save money, and that the pictures, although they looked expensive, had been painted for nothing by a maiden lady who had not been able to get a husband. She had painted the pictures to fit the frames that had been left by a relation in his will.

Wen she told me that she breathed hard and grunted again and smiled and said, "So!"

Then she asked me if I had a money-box, and I said no, and she said, God! she would get me one, and that I should save up all the money I could in order to buy house linen when I got married.

Then she got up and went across the room and opened a cupboard and showed me rows of little money-boxes with labels on them, and she said that they were the money-boxes of the village maidens of B. who were saving money to buy linen when they got married, and that if they had not enough no man would want to marry them. There was another cupboard with money-boxes in which the women who were going to have babies saved up the money to buy clothes for them. She said that no baby was born in B. until its mother had enough money in her box to pay for its clothes and bed and pin-cushion basket. On the bottom shelf of the cupboard were the money-boxes of the babies themselves and a pile of prayer-books with pictures in them of God and the saints, very foreign looking. Whenever a baby was born in B. Frau G. gave it a money-box and a prayer-book, so that it should have a chance of providing for its body and soul.

When she had finished speaking she smiled and grunted and twinkled her eyes again and said, "So!"

I thought I ought to appear interested, and I asked if the babies liked their money-boxes. But Frau G. said that liking had nothing to do with it, that people had to do many things they did not like for their own good, and that everybody's first object ought to be to save, because even a pin saved at the proper time might in the end be the means of saving a life. She didn't say how.

Then she came back and sat down near the table again and said that in England people spent too much money and youth was not disciplined. She said that once, years ago, an English boy had come to B. and put his feet upon her sofa cushions and had spent his pocket-money without asking permission. She had never forgotten it, and she was not surprised at my behaviour in the convent, because ever since she had known that boy she had said that England was not the proper place in which to bring up children. Now that I had come to Germany I should get my religion back again and learn not to argue.

Then she smiled and her eyes twinkled and she said, "So!"

⁂

Frau G.'s villa was on the banks of the Rhine. On one side it had a balcony right over the river, and there was a big shady garden behind with a tiny lake and fountain in it. There were curving mountains on the other side of the water, and a little village with a tiny church in the middle, and a ferry-boat went backwards and forwards between the two banks. The village looked like a toy village from our side and the church like a toy church. I used to lie on the balcony and look across the Rhine and imagine that there were wooden dolls with black hair and bright red cheeks sitting in the cottages and walking up and down the little streets and going into the little church when the bell rang. It rang on Sundays and sometimes in the evenings, and when the air was still the sound came floating right across the river. There were mountains on our side of the river too, and beautiful green fields and valleys.

Frau G. took me for long walks into the mountains. She was never tired. She wore a short net cape and a little black bonnet with strings tied under her chin, and she stumped along quickly in front of me, thumping her umbrella on the ground and wagging her shoulders a little from side to side as she moved. She never went slower even up hill, but when it was very steep she stopped every few minutes and turned to look back for me with her cheeks very rosy and tiny beads of perspiration on her chin. I was sometimes quite a long way behind and she stood and waited for me, and when I came up she smiled and gave a little nod and twinkled her eyes and said, "So!" and then went on again.

Every now and then on the mountain side we came to a little beer-house with a garden in front with chairs and tables where you could sit down to get cool and drink some beer or syrup and eat sandwiches. Whenever we stopped at one the landlord himself always came out and bowed to Frau G. and said, "Good-day, Mrs. Town-Councillor."

And Frau G. said, "Good-day, Mr. Landlord," and pointed at me and twinkled her eyes and said, "This is a little English girl."

Then the landlord bowed again most politely and

said, "Ach, so-o-o? And how does it please you in Germany, Fraulein?"

And I said, "Thank you, well."

Sometimes when we were walking in the mountains we met peasant women coming down the path carrying wood or bundles of some kind. They were always clean and tidy and their faces were kind, though they often looked worn and sorrowful. Frau G. would stop and say, "Good-day, Frau ———. How goes it then at home?"

And they would tell her. If they were in trouble tears came into their eyes as they spoke. Some of them were very poor and toiled hard and had many little children to take care of. Frau G. would always say to them, "Come, then, to my house, and we will see what can be done."

And then when she had stumped on quite a long way and I thought she had forgotten all about it I used to hear her saying to herself, "Gott! Die arme Frau!" ("God! The poor woman!").

And there would be tears in her own eyes as well.

When we walked in the village or on the banks of the Rhine troops of little children would come running to meet us. Some had brown eyes, but most had blue, and they nearly all had round faces and checked pinafores. They kissed Frau G.'s hands and called out all together like little birds piping, "Good-day, Mrs. Town-Councillor!"

And she would say, "Good-day, dear children. How goes it then at school?" or "How much have you in your money-boxes?"

And they would tell her, and her eyes would twinkle and she'd point to me and say, "This is a little English girl."

And they were always pleased and interested. Some of them had never seen a little English girl before, and they would call other children and say to them, "Come quickly! Here is a little English girl!"

And then more would come running up and stand round and look at me.

The little girls would say, "Does one then wear the hair like that in England, Fraulein?"

They meant loose on the shoulders as I had mine.

I said, "Yes."

And they said, "We wear little pigtails."

And then they turned their heads round to show me their little pigtails.

Some of them came behind me and stood on tip-toe and stroked my hair and said, "Ach, how beautiful! Ach, how fine!"

And one tiny girl lifted her baby brother up to me and it stroked my cheek with its soft little hand and said like the others but in a babyish way, "Aie, how beautiful! Aie, how fine!"

After mass on Sunday, while we sat waiting for the

country people to leave the church, the children all came trooping down the aisle together, and when they saw me they whispered to one another, "Look, there's the little English girl," and then they smiled at me, and some made a little bob to me as they went past. I liked to go to mass just to see the children.

On Sunday afternoons we sometimes went for a long walk by the Rhine to a very ancient village where there was an inn with a terrace along the river bank set out with chairs and tables. Many people came to drink beer and chocolate and eat cakes there on Sunday afternoons. Some walked from other villages; some came from the town C. in waggons, and others came across the river in ferry-boats. They were very cheerful. Each family sat round a separate table. There were sometimes an old white-haired grandfather and grandmother, and a younger father and mother, and sons and daughters (a great many) down to tiny children. Each family began to sing as soon as it had had something to eat and drink, and they sang very seriously, as though they had prom-ised to do so and were determined not to stop. Some-times the grandfathers and grandmothers sang too in weak old voices, but sometimes they only smiled and lis-tened and wagged their heads. The fathers and mothers sang loudest and longest. The songs were always love songs. When the young girls had eaten all the cakes they wanted they got up and walked about the terrace between the tables in threes and fours with their arms around each others' waists. Some had thick plaits hanging down behind, and some had coiled their plaits round their heads and placed flowers in them. They had white muslin dresses on and bare arms, and their faces were pink and pretty. I used to think I should like to make friends with them, but I was too shy, because they seemed much more grown up than I. Once when a group was passing our table Frau G. stopped them and said to them, "See, here is a little English girl." And they stopped in a row with their arms intertwined and looked at me with their gentle eyes. I was ashamed to look at them at fist, but afterwards I grew more courageous.

They said, "Is it then beautiful in England, Fraulein?"

And I said, in German, though I was very shy at speaking German to them. "Yawohl! Wunderschön!" ("Yes, rather. Wonderfully beautiful!").

And then I looked down on the ground again, because I knew my eyes were filling with tears. Whenever I thought of England I could see the white cliffs and the grey sea as I saw them when the ship was taking me away.

I did not cry, but the German girls could see how near I was to tears, and they said, cheerfully, "It is right beautiful in Germany too, and when the Fraulein is a little accustomed to it she will love Germany too and no longer be homesick."

I felt grateful to them for speaking to me so kindly and looking at me in such a friendly way. It made me feel less timid about going among the strange girls in the convent. I asked Frau G. if the convent girls would be like these, but she was quite offended. She said that these girls were daughters of the shopkeepers of C., but the girls in the convent were of good family and many of them had titles. I was very sorry.

On Sunday evenings the young men marched through the village to attract the girls to the dancing hall. The young men had straight backs and healthy faces and looked very handsome in their Sunday clothes. The girls came out of the houses and followed them arm in arm, in clean cotton dresses and white stockings, and with smooth shining hair. Once I went and peeped in at the "tanzboden" (dancing-floor), and saw them dancing. The girls looked heavy but very joyful. When the young men wanted the girls to dance with them they beckoned with their heads as much as to say, "Hi! Come over here!" or with their hands, and the girls were not offended but went up to them, and they danced till they were wet with perspiration, and then they stopped and wiped their faces and said, "Gott! Wie mann schwitzt!" ("God! How one sweats!"), and sat down at the little tables round the walls to drink beer and cool down again.

On church festivals big boats full of pilgrims went floating down the Rhine to a holy shrine not far from B.

Some of the pilgrims knelt and prayed and others sang, and red and blue and golden banners waved. When it was a fine day and the sky was blue and the sun shining the boats looked like painted boats in picture-books, and we could hear the pilgrims' voices plainly as they passed the house.

Once I went to see the shrine with a German boy who had come from Berlin to pass his holidays in B. We crossed the river in the ferry boat and walked along the bank on the other side. The German boy was very noisy. As we went along he kept throwing things up into the air and catching them, and running up and down the bank and shouting. He had tight little brown curls and a round face and bright sly-looking brown eyes. He was dressed in a blue alpaca sailor suit trimmed with rows and rows of white braid, and his knickers were very wide and bound with elastic at the knee. He wore a little round straw hat with a bow behind, and a sandwich bag hanging from his shoulder on a long strap. When he had nothing else to throw into the air he threw the sandwich bag. He said that Frau G. was his godmother, and that one of his uncles was a millionaire, and that when they died they would leave him a great deal of money. He said that if I had as much money as he had it would be a good thing for us to marry, because people who had the same amount of money generally did so, that they shouldn't quarrel afterwards about which had most. I said that when I grew up I was going to marry an Englishman. He said that Englishmen were as false as cats, and I was offended. I said that their hair-dressing was much more becoming than Germans' because they didn't make their hair stand up all over their heads like porcupines' quills.

He said, "Das ist ya schneidig" ("But that is smart").

I said I thought it was ugly, and he was offended and said that when he grew up he was going to be an officer and make his hair stand on end, and that many frauleins with lots of money would be glad to marry him, but that if one of them was an English fraulein he wouldn't marry her, because English frauleins had red hair and teeth sticking out in front.

Then we were both offended and ceased speaking. When we got to the shrine we found a large crowd of pilgrims there and lots of little stalls with rosaries and holy pictures on them, and women calling out to everybody that passed to come and buy some. We looked at the stalls and the German boy forgot that we were not on speaking terms and said that all the things were "dummes zeug" ("rubbish"), and that only foolish people spent their money on them. Then we went to look at the famous miraculous statue of the Blessed Virgin that stood in a niche and mended people's arms and legs and cured their illnesses. It was made of wood and looked very old and battered. Its face was an unhealthy yellow colour and there was a crack down one side of its mouth. I did not think much of it. I had seen others that looked much more capable. But you can't go by looks, and when once a person is famous it doesn't make much difference.

There were crutches fastened to the wall and spectacles and medicine bottles which had been left there by pilgrims to show their gratitude for miracles, or sent there when they died or when the doctor said they did not need them any longer. The German boy said that was "dummes zeug" as well, and that the stories of the miracles had been made up for the peasants to believe, because they were too stupid to understand anything else. He said that he did not believe a word of it, but he pretended to, because if he did not his godfather and godmother would not leave him the money they were going to if he did believe.

I had no faith in the miracles either, but I did not tell him so, because I did not like him well enough. I was angry with him for saying that the peasants were so stupid. Other people, who are not peasants, believe in miraculous cures and visions and spirits, and they are not considered stupid. I was sorry for the poor people who had come so far to ask the Virgin Mary to help them. Some of them were old and looked very sad and weak. Many were ill and could hardly walk, but limped along on crutches, or leaning on their friends. Women had brought sick children with them to be cured. One car-

164

ried a baby on a cushion. It lay so still that it looked like a tiny waxen figure. She was sitting alone with it, crying and kissing it, trying to make it wake and look at her. Her tears fell on its face, but it could not hear her or feel her tears. I was sorry for her. I knew the wooden image could not help the baby; but if I had told her so she would not have believed me.

❦❦❦

I promised Frau G. before going to the convent that I would still go to confession and communion as though I had never fallen into the sin of doubt in England. She said that if I did that without questioning I should get my religion back again. But I did not think I should. When you've once got out of the habit of making yourself believe things you can't begin again any more than you can make yourself feel ill again when you've got over the measles. You've had them and they've gone, and you can't get them back again. It's the same about believing things.

The uniform of this convent was a black dress and a black pelerine to wear over the top part of the dress to keep it clean, and a black apron to keep the skirt clean, and black over-sleeves to keep the sleeves clean. Frau G. took me to a tailor to have the things made. It was like getting ready to go to a funeral. I had to have new under-things made as well, because my English ones had too much embroidery on them to wear in a German convent. They put me in danger of the sin of frivolity. I was made to brush my hair tightly back off my forehead and screw it into a little pigtail behind to be insured against the sin of vanity. So I was fairly safe.

It was a very hot morning when we set out for A., where the convent was. I wore my black clothes and a black cape besides, and a black sailor hat, and my pigtail hung down behind. I hated the clothes and they made me dreadfully hot.

A. is a small village with an ancient church and a square market-place and big cobble stones in the street. Some of the houses were black and white and some were grey. There were hills on all sides of it, and on top of the highest we could see the convent.

We arrived in A. just at dinner time and we went into the hotel to have dinner before going to the convent. The waiter showed us into a room with a long table down the middle of it. There were a number of stout gentlemen sitting at the table with their napkins tied round their necks, eating pieces of fat boiled bacon. Some had long glossy beards and some had spiky moustaches, but the backs of all their necks were red and damp with perspiration. I was very surprised to see them; we came upon them so unexpectedly. For a moment they made me think of the knights at King Arthur's table. Frau G. said they were tourists, but I imagined to myself that they had been sitting there for ever eating lumps of bacon fat and never speaking or telling any one where they came from. They did not stop eating or look up from their plates for one instant when we came in, and we sat down at the end of the table and ordered dinner.

After dinner we set out to climb the hill to the convent. I wished Frau G. would not walk so fast, because I was in no hurry to get there. A peasant boy with curly hair and a lame leg pushed my box on a little barrow behind us. It was so hot that he perspired a great deal and he kept stopping every few minutes to take his hat off and wipe his face.

We went up and up, and I began to think we should never reach the top, but at last, when we were all three panting, we came to the convent. It was like climbing up the beanstalk to reach the giant's castle.

There was a broad flight of steps up to the entrance, and there were huge black double doors with iron handles and a grating in the middle. When we rang the bell the grating opened and a big red face looked through and stretched its mouth and showed two rows of large yellow teeth. I thought to myself it was like the face of the giant's cook peeping out through the spy-hole to see if there were a tasty traveller anywhere near to make into a dinner for the giant. But it was a lay sister who only meant to smile at us when she showed her teeth. She did it again when she had let us in, and she made a little bob to Frau G., and said, "Good-day, Mrs. Town-Councillor."

And she smiled again and told the boy with the barrow to put my box down and go into the kitchen for a glass of milk. Then she said that Reverend Mother was waiting for us, and she took us under an archway and across a courtyard into the house and up a lot of stairs and along a corridor into Reverend Mother's room.

It was a small room, but there were big uncurtained windows in each of the four walls. The sun was streaming in at the windows and the room was as hot as an oven. On one side you could see right over the playgrounds and fruit gardens, and all the other land that belonged to the convent, and on the others you could see the hills with woods on them and the valley with a pretty river running through it. There was scarcely any furniture in the room but a table and some wooden chairs and a writing-desk between two of the windows with a big crucifix upon it.

I was very much surprised when I first saw Reverend Mother. I thought I had never before seen any one so broad and tall. Her face was big and red like the lay sister's, with high cheek bones and eyes like bright blue stones, and big sharp teeth growing one upon another in the front. I thought to myself that this room might be the watch-tower of the castle and Reverend Mother the giant's wife on the look-out to stretch her arms through one of the windows and grab hold of a passer-by in case they had nothing to cook for dinner. I should not have been surprised to see the giant come striding in with his club.

Reverend Mother had a very deep, noisy voice, and when she moved she seemed to fling herself about and her skirts and veil whirled round her in the air. But she seemed very kind. She talked a great deal to Frau G., and kept leaving off in the middle to laugh, "ha-ha-ha." It sounded more like a big, cheerful dog barking than a nun laughing. From time to time she stooped down and smiled into my face and patted me on the shoulder, and it felt like being rapped with a cricket bat.

Frau G. and Reverend Mother went on talking together for a long time about all sorts of people I didn't know, and I sat on a chair and wished I could go back to B. with Frau G. instead of staying with strangers in the convent.

At last Frau G. got up to go, and she came over to me and kissed me and took my face between her hands and said, "So! So! Sei ein gutes Kind" ("Be a good child").

I put my arms round her neck and clung to her; but she put them down again and nodded and smiled to me and twinkled her eyes and said, "Goot-pye, goot-pye," and I could see that she had tears in her eyes, although they twinkled. She was sorry to leave me all alone like that. I was afraid I should begin to cry, but I controlled myself and did not give way.

When Frau G. had gone Reverend Mother tried to comfort me. She threw herself about and stooped and looked into my face and went on talking loud and fast in German. I was so irreverent that I could not help imagining that she had suddenly been changed by magic from the giantess into a big black dog, wriggling and bounding and yelping as though it wanted me to play. I tried to put the thought out of my head, but I could not.

She said she would take me to Mother Estelle, who was my dormitory mistress, and we went out of the room and down the stairs and through a great many passages. Reverend Mother kept flinging herself along in front of me and turning her head back over her shoulder to speak and smile at me, and she still reminded me of a big black dog, running down towards a river, looking round and barking and begging me to throw a stone.

At last we turned into a long dormitory with rows of cubicles in it and clean curtains round each one. About half-way down the room we found a cubicle with the curtains drawn back, and inside was a nun on her knees before a little chest of drawers arranging things in it. Reverend Mother said that this was my cubicle and that the nun was Mother Estelle. She introduced us, and smiled and rubbed her hands, and gave another loud and cheerful yelp and threw herself down the dormitory and out at the door. I was glad she was gone, she was so noisy.

Mother Estelle was a very tall nun with a narrow face and a long thin nose, red at the end. She had small round dark blue eyes, set close together, and her forehead was puckered in the middle as if she worried very often; as she really did. There were thirty girls in her dormitory and she had to see that they were tidy and superintend their manners. When I went into the cubicle I saw that she had unpacked my box and was putting my under-clothes away in the little chest of drawers. She looked at each of the things and puckered up her forehead still more and said they were all marked in the wrong place, and that English people always marked their things in the wrong place. It was really the tailor in B. who had made the things and his wife who had marked them. But I did not say so.

Then she shut the chest of drawers and sighed and got up off her knees and showed me a little pin-cushion on the drawers with four safety-pins stuck into it. She said that I must always, at any moment of the day or night, know where each of these safety-pins was, but that I was never to use them except in cases of absolute necessity. She said she had provided the pins for me because I was English. Germans never used pins, but English people had to, because their buttons were always bursting and their strings coming off.

Then she looked at my brushes and combs and sighed again and said that the brushes were much too soft, and that the teeth of the combs were much too close together. She said that English people's combs always had the teeth too close together, because English people never threaded their combs with cotton-wool to keep them clean as Germans did.

Then she puckered up her forehead again and said that she was sorry to have an English girl in her dormitory, because the English never could be taught to do things in the way they ought to do them. They never learnt to walk in the proper way or to enter a room correctly. The real way was to open the door a very little way and to put the right arm and the right leg in first, round the door; then to bring the left leg in between the right leg and the door; then, the right arm and the right leg and the left leg being safely inside the door, the left arm must be brought in and the door handle passed from the right hand to the left hand, and the door shut with the left hand. She showed me how to do it round the left-hand curtain: I thought to myself that if the door opened on the right-hand side one would get one's limbs into a dreadful muddle. But Mother Estelle said that that was the way to make the least draught, and it only needed four moves in all. English people threw the door wide open and came in with all their arms and legs at once. They did not wipe their noses in the correct manner either. The correct way was to grasp the whole nose with the handkerchief and turn the face away; but English people grasped the end which came first, and went on talking just as usual. She said they did not use their soup spoons properly either, and that they were never taught to eat apple tart off the end of their knives as Germans were. I thought I had never heard a nun grumble so much.

When she had finished, she told me that if ever I came out of my cubicle at night when once the lights were out I should be expelled next morning. Then she said that in a short time the girls would begin to arrive and that at five o'clock they would assemble in the big hall and I could meet them there. She asked me if I should like to go and pray in the chapel, but I said, "No, thank you" (I could not have prayed at four o'clock in the afternoon), and she puckered up her forehead and said that, in that case, I must take a book and go and sit in the preparation classroom, and she gave me a book about the lives of the saints and took me to the preparation room. It was a broad gallery that ran right round the top of a big hall with a polished floor. There were rows of desks in threes in the gallery, and you could look down over the balustrade into the hall beneath.

I sat down at one of the desks and felt utterly lost and lonely. At first I looked at the pictures of the saints in the book, but I didn't like them. They were too stout and foreign looking, and they had smooth faces and curled flowing hair. In our books in England the saints had looked hungry and pensive, as they should, seeing how much they had to mortify the flesh. I soon got tired of the book and shut it up and put my arms on the desk and laid my head upon them feeling very sorrowful. Then suddenly I heard a door open in the hall below and footsteps and voices, and when I looked over the balustrade I saw a number of girls in black dresses trooping into the hall, and I knew it must be five o'clock. I got up and went out of the gallery and down the stairs. When I reached the bottom I walked along a passage in the direction of the voices until I reached the door of the big hall. There were crowds of girls in black dresses coming down another staircase that led from the dormitories. Most of them had their arms round one another's necks or waists, and sometimes they stopped and rubbed their cheeks together and kissed, and looked into one another's eyes, and then went on again.

They were all dressed exactly as I was, and all had their hair in plaits, some hanging down behind and some twisted round their heads. Most of them had fair hair and blue eyes, but some had black hair and eyes and brown faces, and a few had red hair and freckles. Some were tall and broad with big hands and feet, but most were small and plump and pink, with curly mouths and chins and bright eyes. They were talking and laughing

174

all together and looking about for their friends, and waving their hands to others in the distance and calling out, "Tag, Lise!" or "Tag, Gretchen," and when two friends met they kissed one another on each cheek and began talking both at once, and then they walked away together with their arms round one another's necks.

I slipped into the hall and sat down on a chair near the door. There were chairs all round the walls and some other girls were sitting alone on them. They were new girls too, but there weren't any other English girls.

Sometimes a group of girls came up to the new ones and stood round them and asked questions. They came up to me and asked questions too. They said, "Wie heisst du?" ("What is your name?"). And, "Woher bist du?" ("Where do you come from?"). And, "Wass ist dein Vater?" ("What is your father?"). And, "Bist du reich?" ("Are you rich?"). And one said, "Bist du adel?" ("Have you a title?").

I was getting used to being asked questions since I had come to Germany. In England we were told not to ask them. When I said I came from London they said, "Gott! Ein grosse Stadt! ("God! A big town!"), and asked if I was English. And when I said yes, they called out to others, "Here's an English girl!"

And then others came up and they all stood round and stared at me without speaking. I stood in the middle and folded my arms behind my back and curled one leg

175

round the other and stood on one foot. I always felt as though I had locked myself up safely somewhere when I stood like that. When they had finished staring they went away again. At seven o'clock a bell rang and we went to a long refectory to have supper of ham rolls and milk and water, and at nine o'clock we went to bed.

Next morning, after mass, we all went out into the playground. Some girls walked up and down in twos and threes with their arms round one another's waists as they had done in the big hall the night before, and some sat on benches and did needlework. Many were crying. They didn't cry to themselves secretly as most people do, but quite loudly, "Ooh-ooh! Ooh-ooh!" and their friends tried to comfort them. As soon as a girl put her handkerchief to her eyes other girls ran up and crowded round her and helped. Sometimes they held smelling-salts up to her nose, and they kept saying, "Gott! Armes Ding! Hat Heimweh!" ("God! Poor thing! She's homesick!").

Soon girls were bursting into tears all over the playground, and their friends ran up to them. It reminded me of the people being taken ill on the steamer and the steward hurrying to take care of them with the basin. One stout girl in a very short skirt with a sandy pigtail and a big flabby face was so noisy that she soon attracted everybody's attention and got the biggest crowd round her.

She kept screaming, "Mamá! Mamá! Ich sterbe! Ich sterbe!" ("Mamá! Mamá! I die! I die!").

And she made her arms stiff and fell backwards on top of the others so that they had to hold her up. Whenever she felt a little better she smiled and kissed them all round, and pulled a big tin of sweets out of her pocket and offered them to everybody and ate some herself; and when she had had enough she put the lid on the tin and the tin back in her pocket and began to cry again. Soon most of the girls were in tears and there were scarcely any left to comfort them.

I was very much surprised. I had never seen so many people crying all at once before. I was inclined to cry myself, but I didn't because I didn't want to be comforted by strangers, and I had not made friends with any of them yet.

Next day we were put into "trios." That meant that the same three girls were made to walk about together or sit together during recreation for a whole week, and not allowed to walk or sit with any other girls. If a nun met a girl standing or sitting alone in the playground she would say, "Where is your trio?"

And then the girl had to go and find the other two. They hated being in "trios," because they always wanted to talk to their "best friends," instead of the girls they were in "trio" with. Sometimes they used to escape from their "trios" and meet their "best friends" in corners, but in a moment a nun would surely come up behind and say, "Where are your 'trios'?" And they had to go back to them.

They used to make secret appointments to have a little talk with their "best friends" in all sorts of odd places, behind doors, in passages, even in the lavatories; but it was no good. They were always found out and separated.

Sometimes a nun would call one of the girls and ask what they had been talking about in her "trio" that day, and later she would call another and ask her the same question in order to see whether the first one had told the truth.

From time to time the girls were sent for to talk with the priest in his room. He lived in the convent and was a very nice man, with long legs and untidy skirts always flapping round them. He had a big hooked nose and kind brown eyes, and his face always looked bright and pleased. He stooped down and looked right into a person's face when he was talking to them. His voice was so high and squeaky that it could be heard coming from a long way off, and one could often hear him talking without seeing him at all.

He used to walk across the playground to say mass in the chapel with his eyes turned up to heaven, his hands folded in his sleeves, his draggled-looking skirts flapping, and the deacon, who was also his manservant, following behind ringing a bell. The girls in the playground always got up and curtseyed and made the sign of the cross when he went by, but his eyes were turned up so far that he didn't see them; but at other times when he came into the playground he was very kind and lively, and he knew no end of little jokes and riddles to make us laugh.

When I went into his room I found him looking at something in a note-book. I think it was the list of "trios" I had been in during the month. He told me to sit down and began to ask me questions about the girls I had been in "trio" with: how I liked them, what I had talked about with them, what they thought about different things, and what I had heard the others talk about together. I could not answer all the questions, because I had not taken much notice of what the others did or said; I didn't know I was supposed to. But he said, never mind, I should do better next time.

Then he said he would like to talk English with me, because the English was a noble and interesting language which he had always wished to master. He said he knew much English literature and had an English newspaper sent to him every week, because he was so much interested in England. He had always wished to visit England, but he had never been able to because he had an invalid brother with whom he spent all his free time, and he could never make up his mind to go so far from him.

Every summer he meant to spend his holiday in England, but when the time came he had not the heart to go.

He asked me the names of many things in English, and when I told him he said, "Gott! Ein interessante Sprache" ("an interesting language"), and wrote it down in his note-book. When his English newspaper came he used to give me the advertisement sheets, and I kept them in my desk, and when I felt homesick I slipped my hand into the desk and touched the paper and remembered that it had come from England and felt comforted.

The other girls were very sentimental. They were always sending long, loving letters home to their fathers and mothers and friends, filled with kisses and little flowers and leaves and locks of hair. They kissed the envelopes when they had addressed them and said, "Darling mamachen," or "Darling papachen," or "darling brother," or "darling little sister."

They had numbers of keepsakes and stacks of photographs in their desks of fathers and mothers and grandfathers and grandmothers and aunts and uncles, and they were always taking them out and kissing each one separately. Many were the portraits of officers their relations. They used to hand them about to the other girls under their desks during preparation and admire each other's officers. They said, "How bold!" "How fierce!"

"How God-like!" "What passionate eyes!" "What a fas-cinating nose!" "What divine moustaches!" Each girl told stories about her own officers to show how brave they were. The girl next to me said that her brother, who was a lieutenant, had hit his orderly in the mouth and knocked some of his teeth out, and that in the evening when they were at dinner the orderly had tried to kill him by breaking a champagne bottle on his head. But the lieutenant had not been frightened. He just jumped up, pulled out his revolver and shot the orderly. Another girl said that her father, who was a general, said that why the English army was so bad was because the officers had no power to punish their men. But I said that En-glish soldiers were so noble-minded that they never needed punishing, and that all they thought about was avoiding going to places where they might be led into temptation. That sounded like boasting, but I should not have said it if they had not spoken first.

Many of the girls had the photographs of their houses, and they showed these too (some were great houses in parks), and said how many rooms they had, and what the furniture had cost, and how many sheets and tablecloths their mothers had; how many guests came to their parties, how much money they would be given when they married, and how rich their "bräuti-gams" (future husbands) would be. Some of the elder girls knew their "bräutigams" already, and the others pretended they did, and told one another secrets about them. All the girls adored babies and flowers and birds, and ate pounds of chocolate. They said everything they liked was "divine" or "*too* sweet." Each girl "schwärmed" for somebody ("schwärming" is something like being in love, but not so serious). Some girls schwärmed for each other, some schwärmed for one of the nuns, some for the doctor. Many schwärmed for the priest, and one or two for the deacon. One even schwärmed for the gardener, though he was very stiff and gouty and had a pimply face. She said a gardener's calling was one of the most poetical. One girl schwärmed so much for another girl that she scraped her initials on her arm with some scissors and filled the scratches with ink to make it look like tattoo. And when she had done so she was afraid she might get blood-poisoning and fainted through fright, and the nuns sent her to the infirmary. One drew a picture of the priest saying mass and kept it in her desk, and whenever she needed a book out of her desk she put her head into it and looked at the picture, and sometimes she cried over it and said, "Gott! Wie sieht er fromm und heilig aus!" ("God! How pious and holy he looks!").

One of the nuns found the picture, but she did not know what it was meant to be. She thought it was a kind of paper puzzle and that when the girl put her head in-

182

side the desk she was trying to solve it with a pencil. It was thrown into the waste-paper basket.

The girl who schwärmed for the gardener did not draw a picture of him (she had not a talent for drawing as the first girl had), but she kept a book about flowers and vegetables in her desk, and said that when she grew up she would be a vegetarian and eat as little meat as possible. She said that though he was a gardener he might have a most romantic nature, and very likely spent his spare time in writing passionate love poems; but dared not say whom he loved for fear of losing his situation.

One holiday I saw a tall stout girl looking through a window at the girl she schwärmed for and wiping the tears from her eyes, and when I asked her what the matter was, she began to cry outright, and said, "It is *too* sweet. My schwärm is wearing a lace petticoat!"

The girl she schwärmed for was pulling up her stocking in the playground so that her lace petticoat was showing, and it made her cry because she thought it so touching.

I was glad when holidays came, because then we went for a walk in the woods outside the convent grounds. The priest walked first of all with his English newspaper, and he would take me out of my "trio" to walk with him and explain to him the words he didn't understand.

All the time he kept saying, "Das ist aber interessant!" ("That is interesting!").

And he kept writing in his note-book and underlining things. Once he began to talk about England. He said that in England there seemed so little supervision and yet the people kept the laws. He said, "Bei uns ging das nicht" ("With us it would not do").

And he began to think about it and pushed his hat on to the back of his head and walked faster, forgetting that he was pulling me along with him.

Some of the girls did not like England and used to talk against it. They said that English ladies could not cook and that was why gentlemen would not marry them and there were so many old maids in England; and that English people only washed their dishes in one water instead of three as Germans did; and that they did not keep their coffee-pots properly clean, or their clothes properly brushed, or their houses properly dusted. They said that every German girl went to a housekeeping class to learn how to keep house and clean and cook.

I said that cooking was not important, but they said that it was and that once a prince had gone to dinner with a general and asked who made the soup, and when he heard it was the general's daughter who had made it he insisted on marrying her, although she was ugly and had no money.

Except on holidays we scarcely moved at all. At recreation, when it was fine, the girls sat round the playground on benches and did crochet work, and when it was wet they walked round the big hall in "trios" and sang, "Deutschland, Deutschland über alles."

I could not get used to it. I felt I wanted to run about and play at something. We had been forbidden to sit still in the English convent. When I said that we had played cricket in England the girls were surprised and shocked. They said that if young girls ran about and became as rough and noisy as boys no gentlemen would want to marry them.

But I didn't care about gentlemen wanting to marry people. Sitting still so long made me feel ill. I used to turn giddy and I lost my appetite. We had pork for dinner nearly every day and salt fish on Fridays. The smell of food made me feel ill. I often had nightmares and I think the other girls had them too, but they said that they had visions. They took their "best friends" into corners in the morning and told them about it. They said their favourite saints appeared to them and made them all sorts of promises. One morning before mass the girl who slept in the cubicle next mine (the girl who had cried so loudly in the playground) called a lot of other girls round her and began telling them about a vision she had had in the night. She said that the Blessed Virgin had come into her cubicle with a pale light all round her and had told her of delightful things that would happen to her. One girl asked if the Blessed Virgin had said anything about a "bräutigam," and she began kissing the others all round and said she had, but that she had told her not to tell the other girls what she had said in case they should be envious. She said that for nothing in the world would she repeat what the Blessed Virgin had said about the "bräutigam," but that he would be very rich and of noble family.

That same afternoon I was very feverish and my head ached terribly. The girls were very kind to me. They all wanted to kiss me and they did everything they could think of to comfort me, until at last a nun came up and said that I must go to the "kranken-haus" (infirmary).

The infirmary was a little house built in a corner of the convent grounds. It had a lot of nice bright rooms in it with beds. There were three girls in bed in the room I was taken to. The doctor was going in just in front of me. The girls were talking and laughing very cheerfully as we went in, but as soon as they saw the doctor they stopped and began to tell him what kind of pains they had. The first girl said, "Oh, God! Mr. Doctor, I have such agony in my stomach."

She had on a little lace cap, and her two yellow plaits were so long they reached half-way down the bed on each side of her. She looked like one of the big baby dolls they sell in the Christmas toy bazaars. She screwed up her face to show the doctor how bad the pain was.

The second girl had a big brown face and a straight nose and white, even teeth. She had pains in her inside too. She kept saying, "Dear Saviour! My stomach hurts so dreadfully."

The doctor said the first girl was to have a compress put on her, and then the third girl began to say, "May I not have a compress too, dear Mr. Doctor? I die of pain."

And then they all began to talk at once and ask if they might have the different things they wanted.

The doctor said, "My dear young ladies, have patience."

And he drew me up to him and sat down and said, "Well, my child, have you pains in your inside too?"

The nun who had brought me told him what was the matter with me, and he began to ask me about the school in London, and the food we had to eat; and he said to the nun it was plain that German school-life did not agree with me. I was having too much white meat and not enough exercise. He said, "This won't do. The child must go back to England."

Then he said I was to go to bed and take a powder, and that he would speak to Reverend Mother about me.

Then he got near the door and said that the other girls were to have nothing more to eat that day and were each to have a big dose of castor oil in the morning.

They began throwing themselves about and crying out, "Ach, weh! Ach nein, Herr Doktor!" ("Oh, woe! Oh, no, Mr. Doctor!").

They reminded me of the fallen angels tossing upon the lake of fire in "Paradise Lost."

But the doctor slipped through the door and got away.

A few days later Reverend Mother sent for me and began dancing round me and booming in her deep noisy voice that I was to leave the convent and to go back for some time to Frau G.'s house to get strong before returning to England. She patted me on the head with her heavy, wooden fingers, and said that she would be very sorry to lose me, and that everybody in the convent would be very sorry. I curtsied and said, "Thank you, Reverend Mother."

The priest shook hands with me a great many times and said that one day he would come to see me in England, and I should take him to see the Houses of Parliament, and I said I would.

The girls were very sorry I was going. They kept on kissing me all day long, and they gave me hundreds of little keepsakes, and I gave them everything I could think of in return. Even Mother Estelle was sorry (although I was English); I had tried to be tidy and polite so as not to worry her.

❖

CHAPTER FIVE

I Find Something to
Believe In

When I got back from Germany I found that I was going
to live with my mother again.* I was very glad. My two
brothers had grown up and gone away and we lived by
ourselves in a house that was small but very pretty. It was
filled with pictures as my uncle's house had been, but it
was small and had not many stairs. In most of the rooms
there was graceful-looking shining furniture called
Chippendale, and there were pretty carpets on the floors
and gay papers on the walls and flowers on the tables.
My mother made any room pretty she went into, and my
grandfather once said that if a room were to have nothing
in it but a few packing-cases and some rags "Cathy"
would make it look charming in a moment. She always
chose books with the brightest and prettiest covers to

*Mrs. Catherine Hueffer, widow of Dr. Francis Hueffer.

189

put in front of the shelves in the bookcases and put the ugly ones behind, even if they were learned. She said it was quite easy to get them out if you wanted to, and the bookcases glowed and gleamed like great big jewels.

My mother was very pretty. She had fair hair and an absolutely straight nose, and a nicely shaped mouth with beautiful even white teeth, and her eyes were a bright clear blue. When I came home from Germany she looked sad and wore a black dress. If any one began to tell her something that sounded like bad news her eyes would grow frightened in an instant, and her face would look strained and anxious until she found out that nothing really serious was the matter. That was because so many people she loved had died within the past few years: my father, and my grandfather, who was her father, and my grandmother, who was her mother, and my aunt, who was her half-sister; and she always seemed to be afraid that other people were going to die. She had loved her father and mother better than anything in the world. When she spoke of my grandmother the tears always came into her eyes, and when my grandfather was mentioned she sighed and said, "Ah, dear! Poor papa!" When people told her of misfortunes that had happened to themselves or others her face looked sorrowful and her mouth grew lined with pain, even if she didn't know them. But when she heard of other people's good fortune she looked just as proud and joyful as if it had happened to herself. She would go off at once to any distance to help a person, no matter who it might be, even if she did not like them very much. She would sit up night after night to nurse a friend, or a servant, or anybody who was ill, and never complain and say she was tired next day. If people came into the room when she was sitting in a comfortable chair she would get up at once and make them take the best chairs and she herself would take the worst and say, "I always like a hard chair. It's better for my back." And if she had fruit or sweets or anything nice to eat she would give it all to the first person she met and say, "You take it. It really isn't good for me. I'm only eating it because I don't want it to be wasted." She was always ready to give up anything she had to any one who wanted it. But if she saw a big boy beating a little boy she would rush out to stop him. If she heard of a strong person ill-treating a weak one her face would grow red and her eyes would shine and she would be nearly as furious as my grandfather used to be, and she'd say, "I *hate* injustice." If she had ever met a tyrant tyrannising she would most certainly have attacked him. She was rather timid on her own account, and afraid of things like mad dogs or drains or men who looked rough or as if they had bad characters. But if she was protecting some one weaker than herself she was afraid of nothing. She didn't much like being contradicted because, she said, "I never insist upon anything unless I'm *positively certain*." And when people proved to her that she was wrong she would look exceedingly surprised and say, "It's most extraordinary!"

When she was a girl she had painted some very beautiful pictures which had been admired by famous artists, and placed in exhibitions, and nearly always sold. But she couldn't give much time to painting because there was always some one ill or in trouble, or who wanted taking care of. At first she took care of her father and mother and her brother Oliver, who was said to be a genius. When she was married she took care of my father and her children and her house and servants and a lot of other people besides, and then she gave up painting altogether. Sometimes when she was telling me about it her face would look wistful and she'd sigh and say, "It *did* seem a pity!" But then she'd correct herself immediately afterwards and say she thought perhaps she had been happier taking care of other people than painting pictures.

When I got back to England I was growing a big girl. I kept my hair in a pigtail as I had worn it in Germany and had all my dresses let down. But I had not got my religion back. The discipline had made me tidy, but it did not give me faith. When I had thought it over I knew that why I had found it so difficult to believe in religious things was because I'd only been told to do so by other people, who had also been told to do it by other people, and so on. They'd none of them had any proof or anything to show for it. And the people who had taught me did not look particularly clever. They said that what they taught had been revealed by God. But other people said God had revealed just the opposite and that the first people believed wrong and would be punished for it. Mr. Hall, the most pious of the cabmen in the mews near my grandfather's house, would have said that the Pope and the saints and the priests and the nuns were thorough bad lots, and they would have said that he was doomed. And they would both have said that the Jews and Turks and other heathens "stank in the face of God" (that was a sentence in one of Mr. Hall's sermons). And the Jews and Turks and other heathens would have scorned them back and said they were unclean and didn't have their food cooked in the proper way. It's very puzzling, and it makes it very awkward for the Lord, because they are all certain that He is on their side and expect Him to punish the other people. I asked my mother what she thought about it, and she sighed and said, "It was quite true, and the same in *everything*, not only religion." She said, "If *only* people wouldn't disagree so much! It would make it better for everybody."

But having nothing at all to believe in somehow used to worry me. Before I went to the convent, when I had been an anarchist, I had believed in punishing tyrants and getting up a bloody revolution to make everybody happy. Believing in nothing at all is like walking up a long staircase with no bannisters to hold on to.

One day a grown-up young lady came to see me. She was the elder sister of one of the Protestant girls in the English convent. She was very tall and slim and she stooped rather, and she was very fashionably dressed. She had a long light brown face, not quite straight, and large black eyes that protruded slightly. They did not look very kind or clever but empty and bright, and as if they did not see very far. Two of her teeth stuck out just a little in the front, but not enough to be really ugly. She had a moist-looking mouth that smiled rather often, smiles of different sizes. Some were quite tiny smiles, some were a little bigger, and when they were biggest you saw her teeth quite plainly. She sat in an armchair opposite to me and talked and her arms and legs looked very long and tired.

She said that since she had been grown up she had been going into society, but that now she had left off going there. She said that people in society were frail and unprincipled and did disgraceful things. Some of the things they did were to bleach their finger-nails, and have their faces skinned at great expense to make themselves young and beautiful, and sit in dark rooms waiting for the agony to pass. And afterwards, if they were not as young and beautiful as they thought they ought to be, they refused to pay the bill and went to law. She told me a lot of other things they did, but I have not got room to put them all down here. She said that all the people in society hated and despised one another for not having something they ought to have or for not doing something in the way they ought to do it (just like religious people), and that all they thought about was rushing from place to place in search of feverish amusement, ruining one another's reputations and taking care that other people should not find out how bad they were themselves. She said that she had written an article about it exposing them, but it had not been published. Then she took a very big pair of spectacles with deep black rims out of her pocket and put them on. Her fingers looked very thin while she was doing it and the glasses made her eyes swell out and look like dark muddy pools. Then she smiled a small smile and said that when she first went into society people had told her that if she put on nice clothes and stood about for long enough in a sufficient quantity of drawing-rooms some gentlemen would in the end be certain to want to marry her; but that she had stood about in a great many drawing-rooms for a long time, and although several gentlemen had looked from a distance as though they would like to marry her, when they had come nearer and been introduced they hadn't wanted to any longer. Then she smiled a medium-sized smile and said that she was not sorry the gentlemen had not wanted to marry her, because since she had left off going into society she had been studying and thinking deeply, and had little by little been drawing nearer to perfect truth. I was very interested. It sounded just what I was looking for, and I asked her to explain it to me. She said that it was difficult to explain to any one who had never studied it, but that, combined with perfect beauty, it was in everything around us if only we had the perception to perceive it. If we put ourselves into a proper frame of mind and sought it earnestly we could not fail to find it. Sometimes it gradually became apparent, and sometimes it was suddenly apprehended in an illuminating flash of light. It was really the same thing as the Immense Reality. I asked her who had found out about it, and she said that it had been revealed by the Master Mind which was the same thing as the Omnipotent Reasoner, or the Supreme Will. She said that she had written an article about that too, but that it had not been published.

I said it sounded very difficult to understand and that I should like to have it properly explained. She said that she could take me to some places where very wise and learned people were giving explanations. Some did it for five shillings, some for half-a-crown, and some for less. Some charged a great deal, as much as a guinea, and they were the cleverest and wisest of them all.

On the following Sunday we went to a small house in a fashionable quarter. We went up the steps into the passage, and a long, thin lady in a tight black dress, with a tiny head and light eyes and no chin, with shining black cherries in her hat, who was selling literature stopped me in the entrance. She seemed to think I was too young to go in and asked me if I had ever seen anybody under control. I said, "Oh, yes; often." I thought to myself that all the girls at school had been under control, and servants, and everybody else who had to do as they were told. She did not mean that, but I thought she did. Then the grown-up young lady paid her five shillings for each of us and she let us pass.

We went into a room on the right-hand side of the passage. It looked out on to a garden. At the top of the room there was a platform with a desk upon it, and there were rows of chairs across the middle of the room. The window and the walls had purple hangings. A middle-sized lady was sitting at the desk on the platform. She had dark yellow hair and pale greeny-grey eyes that moved about very quickly and sandy eyebrows. Her face was heavy and sallow and looked business-like, but not healthy. She was a spiritualist lady. She was counting up little heaps of pennies that were standing in a row on the ledge of the desk and putting them into a silk bag with strings. There were a lot of other ladies sitting on the chairs. They all looked expensively dressed. They wore fur coats and fashionable hats, and most of them had pink trustful faces and wide-open eyes. Many of them had on pearl necklaces and you could see the little clasps of them just inside the collars of their coats when they pushed them back. The lady at the desk was so busy counting up the pennies that she took no notice at all of them, but they were all staring hard at her as though they thought that what she was doing was very important. When she had finished counting the pennies she tied up the bag and rang a little bell and said that now the sitting would begin. Then she got off the platform and went to a chest on the left-hand side of the room and took out a white robe like a nightgown, and put it on and tied it in round the waist with a string, and the other ladies stared hard at her all the time. Their eyes seemed to roll round after her all together as if they were only one pair. The spiritualist lady went back to the platform and said she would give her usual Sunday morning address, and that afterwards she hoped to go "under control" for a little while, and then perhaps there would be some interesting messages from our spirit friends. She had rather a sharp, grating voice, not at all pleasant or friendly. She passed her hand across her forehead and wore a dreamy, far-away look, and said that she could feel the presence of many spirit friends that morning, waiting to give us messages of hope and comfort. She was just going to begin the address when she remembered that she had not locked up the bag with the pennies in it, and she pulled up the white robe and took a key out of the pocket in her skirt underneath and locked the desk and put the key back into her pocket. Then she passed the back of her hand over her forehead again and began the address.

She said that while we were in the material world what we must be most careful to do was to keep our bodies in good condition for the sake of any of our spirit friends who might wish to use them for demonstrating their presence to their dear ones who were still on this side of the veil. We must take care always to keep ourselves well fed on good and nourishing food and to spend time on the consideration of our clothes, because when we were well fed and dressed our minds possessed a certain peace and satisfaction which they couldn't possess if we were badly dressed and under-nourished, and that that feeling of bodily satisfaction was essential to our spiritual welfare. The ladies in the audience looked at one another and nodded their heads as if they thought that what she was saying was quite true. Then she said what a terrible disappointment it would be to any spirit revisiting this earth with the best and most affectionate intentions to find itself lodged in a body that was worried and nerve-racked through want of proper food and clothing. Such a state of things would not be fair either to ourselves or to our dear ones that had passed, and we must take great care to avoid it, otherwise we could not hope to do our duty to ourselves or to our friends either on this side or the other. She said some other things as well, but that was the longest part, and the part which the ladies liked best and which was easiest to understand.

Then she began to pass the backs of her hands over her forehead again and look wild and worried and she said she could feel the approach of spirit control. She said that as the control always took so much out of her she was obliged to have two professional ladies present to massage her when she felt that she was getting overcome. Then two ladies came up and sat in two chairs just below the platform facing the audience. They were the professional ladies. They looked severe and took off their gloves and rolled back their sleeves, and the ladies in the audience glanced at one another again and nodded and raised their eyebrows.

Then the spiritualist lady rubbed her forehead again and said that she would like some music to obtain the most favourable possible atmospheric condition, and a plump rosy lady sitting at the end of the row in which I was with a hurdy-gurdy on a table in front of her began to turn the handle to grind a tune. She was dressed in black, but a filmy fashionable sort of black, and she had little diamond ear-rings in her ears. She was pinker and plumper than anybody else and looked soft and good to eat, like a nice cream pudding. She was staring so hard at the spiritualist lady that her eyes looked as if they would start out of her head, and her mouth was a little open. Then the spiritualist lady got down from the platform with her eyes shut and her arms spread out and began to sway about the room and bump against the furniture. The grown-up young lady whispered to me that this was a most solemn moment and that she was in a trance and under the control of spirits.

Some of the spirits were English, and some were Irish, and some were Scotch, and some were of other nations, and whichever spirit it was controlling her made her speak with its own particular accent. They all seemed to be in great trouble, or as if they couldn't stand the climate, and she began to groan and scream most sadly.

She said, "Oh, it's so da-a-a-rk! I can't se-e-e!" And, "Oh! it's co-o-o-ld! I'm tre-e-e-e-mbling!" and then she stood still for a moment for us to see her trembling. Then she went on wriggling again and throwing her arms about and turning round on her heels and doing a great many other very peculiar things.

When the spirits found out that it was no use complaining and that they would have to make the best of things, they began to settle down a little and wonder where they were, and ask to have things properly explained. When it was a Scotch spirit it said, "Where am I? Oh! A dinna ken! A dinna ken!" When it was Irish it said, "Och! begorra, phwere the divvil am I got to?

Phwill ye tell me, plaze?" And when it was a French one it said, "Ah, I implore you, vill you 'ave ze kindness to tell me vere I find myselves?"

The ladies in the audience kept whispering together, and one of them, a stout elderly lady in the front row, kept saying to the spirits, "Don't be frightened. No one will hurt you. You are among good, kind, loving friends."

The lady with the hurdy-gurdy went on grinding out the proper sort of tune. When it was time for the spirit to change she touched a spring and ground a different one. When the spirit was Scotch she played "*The Bonnets of Bonnie Dundee*." When it was Irish she played "*Kathleen Mavourneen*," and when it was French she played the "*Marseillaise*."

She still looked dreadfully frightened, as though she might be going to make a mistake in the music. She seemed to be clinging on to the hurdy-gurdy with fear. But she couldn't have made a mistake really, because she had a little programme written in pencil with the list of tunes she was to play spread out on the hurdy-gurdy in front of her, and the right sort of spirit always came to the music she played, just as though it had all been properly arranged beforehand.

At last the spiritualist lady gave a loud and awful groan and fell back into an armchair that had been put ready for her to do it in between the two professional ladies, and they began to stroke her head and wipe the perspiration from her brow and rub her arms and hands and feet very professionally. She was still wriggling and groaning and they kept comforting her and saying, "It's all right now, dear! There's nothing to fret about. You've done us all a great, *great* service, and we're very, *very* grateful to you. There! You're better now!"

Then they frowned and said she really did too much in her anxiety to be helpful to others, but it took it out of her dreadfully, and her friends were not going to be selfish.

Then the spiritualist lady left off groaning and said she was beginning to feel better, and she sat for some time with her face hidden in her hands, shivering a little and giving a sudden jerk from time to time, and while she was doing that the lady who had played the hurdy-gurdy went round with a plate and made a collection.

When she had finished the spiritualist lady recovered and said there was still time for a few cases of special investigation, and would any one who desired spiritual help come up and sit in the front row.

Only one lady besides myself and the grown-up young lady remained. It was getting near lunch-time and the rest seemed to melt away like magic. The grown-up young lady said that if it had not been so near a meal time a great many more would have required spiritual help, and she told me to go and sit beside the other lady in the front row and see what the medium would say to me. We sat side by side and the spiritualist lady sat in front of us.

The lady next to me was very small and thin, but she looked as though she must be very rich. She had a little, anxious, pointed face, quite covered with tiny lines and wrinkles, and pale grey hair beautifully waved with curling-tongs, and a long black lace veil on her hat. Her eyes looked very sad and wistful.

She said to the medium in a little gentle voice, "Have you any message from my son to-day?" And the spiritualist lady shut her eyes and passed her hands across them and said, "Yes . . . it is growing clear. . . . I can see distinctly. . . . Give me your hands."

And the lady put her tiny little hands covered with sparkling rings into the medium's, and I could see them tremble. She said, "Are you here, Ronald, my son?" And the medium answered as though it was the lady's son speaking, "Yes, mother." The lady said, "Is it well with you, my dear?" Her voice was trembling too. The son said, "Yes, mother, but I miss you very much. I wish you were here with me." And the lady whispered, "My darling boy!"

Her face was shining as though she could really see her boy and were close to him. She seemed to have forgotten that anybody else was there. She didn't speak for a few moments. She seemed to be looking and looking at her boy, too happy even to want to say anything to him. And at last she said, "Can you see me, Ronald?" And the son said, "Yes, mother, but I cannot show myself to you yet. Some day I shall be able to." And she said in a very low voice, "Yes, yes, I know, I'm waiting. . ." Then after another few moments she said, "It will be your birthday in a few days. You will be nineteen. I shall be thinking of you . . ." And the medium said, as though it were the son speaking, "Come again soon, mother. Come as often as you can. It's such a help to me." And she said, "Yes, yes, my dear, I will."

Then the medium let go of the lady's hands and she dropped her veil over her face and went away out of the room on tiptoe, like a shadow, without making the slightest sound. We did not move till she had gone, and then the medium drew her chair in front of mine and took hold of my hands and shut her eyes and said, "L— L— Can you think of anybody whose name begins with L?" I said yes, that we had had an undernurse called Louisa when I was quite a little girl, before my father died. The spiritualist lady looked cheerful and said, "Yes, yes, Louisa. That's the name I'm trying to get. I can see her quite plainly. She's standing close beside you. It is evidently your nurse, because she has on a white cap and apron. She is stooping down with her hand quite near the ground, raising it higher little by little. She means to say, 'What a big girl you have grown,

Miss, since I saw you last.' She is smiling and raising her arms to show how pleased and surprised she is that you have grown so much."

But Louisa wasn't dead at all. She had been to see me only the week before, and she was coming the following week as well. Even if she *had* died in between she couldn't have been very much surprised to see how much I had grown in a week. But I didn't say so. I just said, "Thank you very much." Then she said that she had seen at once that I was very psychic and that I ought to attend the meetings regularly in order to develop my gifts. I said, "Thank you," again, and we came away.

When we got outside the grown-up young lady asked me whether I had liked the meeting. I said not very much because the spiritualist lady had not explained any of the things I wanted to know about, and the spirits had not said anything really interesting. She was offended. She said it was because I had not put myself into the proper frame of mind, and that she herself had derived great spiritual consolation from the meeting and had greatly added to her store of knowledge.

A few days later she took me to another meeting, but not in a fashionable quarter. It was in a big house in a gloomy street and it had "Bedroom to let for single gentleman" written on a card in the window on the right-hand side of the door. We went into the passage and paid a shilling each to a gentleman with crooked eyes and a husky voice who had some literature in a basket hung round his neck.

The grown-up young lady said that the meetings held in this house were considered particularly good, and that the gentleman who conducted them was a celebrated medium who had been the bosom friend and spiritual adviser of another celebrated gentleman who wrote in the newspapers. I felt very interested and glad that I was going to see him, and we went into the room.

He was a tiny man with black hair and small bright eyes and a yellow face and dirty finger-nails. He seemed to be darting about all over the room talking to the people. When we came in he darted over to us and shook hands with us and said, " 'Ow do you do, young ladies? I'm very glad to see you. Will you come and sit near the fire or will you find it too 'ot?"

We sat on chairs near the door and waited twenty minutes for the meeting to begin. There were a lot of people sitting round the room on chairs and on a low wide sofa against the left-hand wall. Some looked rich, but some were poorly dressed and looked quite ordinary. There were several gentlemen in skimpy suits with damp hair and dull eyes and pasty faces, and one elderly gentleman with white hair and moustaches, and a red forehead and blue irritable-looking eyes.

One gentleman in a skimpy suit, a young gentleman, was the celebrated medium's assistant. He told us that at eight o'clock punctually the doors would be closed and the celebrated medium would go into a trance under the control of an Egyptian spirit called Jumbo, who had been mangled and boiled alive hundreds of years ago. He said that one evening the Egyptian spirit had quite unexpectedly given a description of the exact sensations he had experienced while being boiled and that the audience had considered it most striking and interesting.

At eight o'clock the door was shut and the celebrated medium turned down the gas and sat down in an armchair underneath the gas bracket. He closed his eyes and folded his hands and jerked first one shoulder and then another. That was to show that he was going into a trance. Then he suddenly began to speak in an awfully deep voice, much deeper than the one he had spoken to us in. It was really the Egyptian spirit, Jumbo, speaking. The Egyptian spirit said that he had often been asked by seekers after the truth on this side for some description of the life beyond the grave, and that now he was going to give them in a few words some of his own experiences. He could safely say that the life beyond the grave was a 'appy life, supposing that our conduct on this side of the grave had been such as to entitle us to 'appiness on the other. He said that some spirit friends were discontented for a bit and found that that life was not all they could wish that life to be. Some spirit friends was actually violent when they first come across and even used bad language, but they was soon brought to reason by other spirit friends what knew the truth and taught that the path of love was the path to 'appiness, and then they settled down. He said that some friends on this side was anxious to 'ave a glimpse of everyday life on the other side, and wanted to know whether there was streets and 'ouses on the other side like there was on this. He was there to tell them that there was, and that walking down the street on the other side was very similar to walking down the street on this. There was 'ouses along both sides of the streets with windows in them, though it was a curious fact that many of the 'ouses 'ad no doors. There was 'angings in the windows just as there was in the windows on this side, and there was 'angings on the walls as well. But the difference was that you could pass your 'and right through the 'angings on the other side and feel nothing and make no impression on them at all. He said that was a strange and interesting fact that had repeatedly been taken notice of.

When he had got as far as this there was a knock at the street door and the assistant jumped up and said below his breath, "Room full!" and went towards the door of the room. But the celebrated medium suddenly said in his own voice, though he didn't have to come out of the trance to do it: "There's room for one on the sofa."

And so there was. And the assistant went out and opened the street door and came in again followed by a very tall stout lady shabbily dressed in black. She had a broad round face and bright blue eyes and a big friendly smile. She walked across the room on tiptoe with long steps so as not to disturb the other people, and kept saying, "Very sorry, I'm sure," and she sat down heavily on the end of the sofa which gave an awful creak, and the other people on it had to huddle close together because she took up much more room than any ordinary person.

The celebrated medium was still in a trance waiting to go on with the address, but she didn't know he was, and she kept nodding to people in a very friendly way and saying, "Good evening to you," and then she began to explain how it was that she had come so late. She said she had got off the very minute she had finished washing up the supper things, but that she had had to keep waiting about for 'busses, which does keep anybody back so.

When the celebrated medium saw that the other people were listening to her instead of waiting for Jumbo to go on with the address, he came out of the trance and turned up the gas. The stout lady went on talking, and the other people were interested. She said that, though they might not think it, she and her family were in great trouble, and that a kind lady had given her a shilling and paid her bus fare from Hammersmith, where she lived, and told her to come here, for she would be certain to find help. She said that she was the mother-in-law of a burglar, but that he was not really a burglar, but had been falsely accused. She said he was as straight and steady a man as ever walked the earth. Why the police thought he was a burglar was because they had caught him with a big bag full of burglar's tools one foggy night. What had really happened was that he had been for a walk with some friends who had bad characters and they had shoved the bag into his hand and took theirselves off when they see the coppers coming round the corner. If he had had the sense to drop the bag and run it never would have happened, it being so foggy. But he never see the coppers till they was close upon him. He had since written heart-breaking letters on blue paper from the prison begging his little ones to be careful whom they played with in the street, because his own misfortune was entirely due to the keeping of low company. The mother-in-law said that, in this case, as in every other, the wife and children suffered most, and what to do to help her daughter and the little ones to get a bit of food she sometimes did not know. There were four of them and the twins were still in arms, as you might say. She had often thought that if she could have had a bit of a talk with her dear old grandfather, who had died five years ago at seventy-nine, it would have done her a world of good. She had lived along of him before he died and was the very spit of him except for being taller. She had never known him fail her when it was a matter of giving good advice. She said he was a fine old gentleman, and excepting for a hasty temper and being a trifle near, for which nobody could blame him, hadn't got a fault. He was that saving and economical that any one could scarcely credit it, and when once a lady had bought him a pair of brand new boots, instead of getting them for him on the instalment system at the rag-shop, as he used to do himself, he kept them inside the bottom of his bed and covered them up carefully with the sheets and blankets in the day time for fear any one should steal them from him, and went on wearing his old ones though his feet was on the ground. And when the lady came to see how he liked his new boots she thought at first that he had pawned them when she saw him wearing the old ones, but he pulled back the bedclothes and showed her the boots lying side by side, safe and comfortable, all black and shining like a nigger woman's twins. And the lady was so pleased to see them there that she promised to buy him a new pair when they were worn out. The burglar's mother-in-law said she wasn't going to sit there and say the old man never took a glass, because it wouldn't be the truth. But he never paid for one himself and never drank unless he was invited. The lady who had given her the shilling had told her that she could be put into touch with the spirit of her grandfather if she came here, and since she heard the words she felt she couldn't keep away.

The people in the audience were all extremely interested, and one very old lady with thin white hair and a shaking head pointed to the celebrated medium and said, "This gentleman can help you," and the burglar's mother-in-law nodded and smiled at him and said, "I should take it very kindly, sir, I'm sure."

Then the celebrated medium shut his eyes and jerked his shoulders one by one again and waited a few minutes and then said in a dreamy manner, "What? yes . . . yes . . . it's growing clearer . . . no, I can't see . . . yes, I can . . . I see the figure now quite plainly . . . it is that of an aged man . . . with white 'air . . . of somewhat stout build . . . with blue eyes . . . and a cheerful countenance . . . with a good deal of colour in 'is cheeks . . . 'is nose is on the fleshy side, and somewhat swollen. . . ."

The burglar's mother-in-law was nearly struck dumb with astonishment. She said, "If that ain't gran'pa to the life!" And she looked all round the room at the other people with her eyes wide open, and she said, "You could knock me down with a feather! I wouldn't never have believed it if I hadn't heard it! It's gran'pa to the life!"

Then the celebrated medium said in a still dreamier voice, "He seems to be pointing . . . pointing downwards . . . towards his feet . . . He is trying to tell me something . . . but I can't quite understand what he means."

The burglar's mother-in-law was quite excited, and

she said, "Well, I can tell what he means then, if you can't. He means them very boots I was a-telling you about. That's what he means, right enough."

Then she looked all round the room again and said, "I wouldn't never have believed it if I hadn't heard it. *Never!*"

Then the celebrated medium said, "He seems to be trying to communicate to me some word that begins with G. . . . I can't quite get it. . . . He seems impatient that he is not understood immediately . . ."

And the burglar's mother-in-law said, still quite excited, "He would be! That's him all over! Didn't I say he was hasty-tempered? It's gran'pa he's a-trying to say. That's what that is, right enough. Well, I never! Who'd have thought it possible?"

I never saw any one so much astonished.

Then the celebrated medium wriggled and stretched out his hands, and some one in the audience said to the burglar's mother-in-law, "Put your hands in his and perhaps you will get a message from your grandpapa."

And the burglar's mother-in-law tiptoed across the room again, full of joy and excitement, and put her hands in the celebrated medium's, and he said as though it was the burglar's mother-in-law's grandfather speaking, "Is it you, grand-daughter?"

And she said, "Yes, it is, gran'pa. It's Ellen." And the gran'pa said, "Thank you for coming to see me, grand-daughter." And she said, "I'd have come a jolly sight sooner, gran'pa, if I'd have known you was so handy. I only wish I had." And the gran'pa said, "I know you are in trouble, Ellen, and I'm very sorry to know it. And I'm very sorry for the wife and them poor little children."

And the burglar's mother-in-law said, "You're right. Can you give me any notion, gran'pa, what I ought to do to help them? She goes out working by the day, poor girl, but it don't bring in much. I mind the children while she's gone. Can you think of anything I could do to help them, gran'pa?"

And the grandfather said, "Yes, I can, Ellen. This is what you've got to do. Remember that I am always near you, watching over you, and don't worry. When things seem to be at their worst they'll mend and be put right. Don't you trouble your 'ead about anything. It will all be for the best in the end. There was a meaning in it."

And she said, "Thank you, gran'pa, I'll try to think so. And it will be a powerful sight of comfort to know you're watching over us. Can you tell me something more, gran'pa?"

And he said, "Be careful, Ellen, when you are taking them twins across 'Ammersmith Broadway in the per-ambulator. It's a nasty bit, that there, and my 'eart's often been in my mouth when I've been watching you. Go slow, Ellen, go slow. Put 'em in the pram by all means if they're too 'eavy to carry, but be careful 'ow you go."

She said, "You're right, gran'pa, you are indeed. I'll be careful."

And the grandfather said, "Good-bye, Ellen; I must go now. Come again soon, Ellen, and don't forget I'm always waiting for you."

And she said, "That I will, if I have to pop my wedding ring to do it."

And she tiptoed back across the room with a happy face and said when she sat down, "If I didn't take them blessed twins across the Broadway in the pram this very morning! I never would have believed it if I hadn't heard it with my own ears, *never!*"

And she sat down in her place again and kept nodding her head in a surprised way to herself as though she were still saying to herself that she never would have believed it.

Then the celebrated medium began to describe other spirits that he could see standing or sitting about the room. Some were old, some middle-aged, and some quite young. One was a little baby lying in a lady's lap. Nobody could see them except the celebrated medium, but he said he could. The old gentleman with the irritable-looking eyes asked if there was an Indian among them, because he wanted to be put into touch with a Hindu gentleman whom he had known. And the celebrated medium said that there *was* an Indian standing quite close to him, evidently very much interested in him. He said, "He has some long bright-coloured feathers in his 'air and the scars of wounds and scratches on his cheeks, and he is brandishing a war-like weapon like a tomahawk."

The old gentleman was offended. He said his friend was a wise and learned Hindu, a great scholar, and that he would never dream of putting feathers in his hair and scratching his face and brandishing a tomahawk. The celebrated medium was a little offended too. He said that Indians was Indians all the world over and was not like us, and you could never tell what members of them black, uncivilised races might not take it into their 'eads to get up to. The old gentleman got quite angry and answered back and said that it was ridiculous to confound a learned Hindu with an American Red Indian.

The meeting broke up soon after that, and the celebrated medium told me as we went out that he had seen as soon as I came into the room that I was extremely psychic, and that I ought to develop my gifts by attending the meetings regularly.

I went to a good many other meetings, but they did not do me any more good than the first two had done. They were all alike. The mediums all gave the same sort of addresses and then said the spirits were in the room, and the audience believed they were because the medium said so. But no one else ever saw them. A good many spirits came to see me and gave me messages, but

I couldn't understand them, and didn't know who the spirits were. When I said so the mediums were offended and said coldly, "I am sorry to be so unsuccessful." The grown-up young lady was offended too, and always said it was because I did not put myself into a proper frame of mind. I felt like a naughty girl at school, but I couldn't help it. I didn't know what the proper frame of mind was or how to get into it, but she said it was because I set my face against it and didn't want to know and understand. She said, as the nuns had said, that what I lacked was faith. When once I had faith I should find it easy to believe in and understand about Perfect Truth and Perfect Love and the Immense Realities and all the other great and important things I wanted to understand. If she and all the other people at the meetings did not have faith they would never be able to believe in all the things that happened at the meetings, but would live in darkness and be in the same unhappy position in which I was myself. She wasn't kind and sorry for me as the nuns had been when I didn't believe in going to hell, but angry and irritable. At last she said that she would write an article about that too, explaining everything, called the "*Absolute Essentiality of Faith*" (I think that was what she said it would be called), and that when it was published I should read it and then perhaps I should understand. I said, "Thank you very much." I didn't want to argue because she was so easily offended.

Some of the people told me that they had been to meetings where the spirits really appeared, but only under very favourable circumstances. They would not show themselves unless everything had been properly prepared. I said I should like to go to some of those meetings, but they said that I must not, because I was too young and inexperienced. The spirits at those meetings were sometimes a very mixed and shady lot, and there were some shocking characters among them that needed keeping in their places with a firm, strong hand. If you happened to be present when they "materialised," they might take a fancy to you and make your life a perfect misery. One lady told me that a very bad spirit had taken a fancy to her, and that whenever she went out to dine it stood upon the doorstep of the house and kept on knocking loud double knocks at the street door, and when the servants opened the door there was no one there and they were offended and threatened to give notice. Since then she had never dined out in comfort, because even when it wasn't knocking she thought it was and imagined she heard it, and it made her nervous and spoilt the taste of everything she ate. She said there were some incorrigible practical jokers among the spirits who never understood when they had gone far enough.

It all sounded very strange and funny. I couldn't understand why the dead should want to come to speak through the mouths of people like the spiritualist lady or the celebrated medium. They never seemed to choose people who looked gentle and well educated. All the mediums I saw had the same hard, empty faces and common way of speaking. Not one of them looked as though they could be liked or trusted. And when I thought of my grandfather speaking to me through the mouth of the celebrated medium with his dirty finger-nails in that common room with the ugly gas bracket in front of all the people as the burglar's mother-in-law's grandfather had done, or mixing with the shady lot of spirits and the incorrigible practical jokers that stood on doorsteps and knocked run-away double knocks just for spite, I felt that it was all impossible, and I gave up going to the meetings.

But I still felt anxious to have something to believe in.

Then one day my eldest brother* came to stay with us. He was a fair, clever young man, rather scornful, with smooth pink cheeks and a medium-sized hooked nose like my grandfather's, a high, intellectual forehead, and quiet, absent-looking blue eyes that seemed as if they were always pondering over something. I was nervous with him, because he was very critical and thought that nearly every one was stupid and not worth disagreeing with. But he was very kind and liked to take me out to tea. He wore a black coat with a cape over the shoul-

*Ford Madox-Hueffer.

ders, and when we took hands and walked along it floated out a little way behind.

Once he took me a long way to see a famous gentle-man* who lived outside London. His house was quite a plain-looking little house, and when we went in there were a lot of people sitting round the table in a tiny dining-room having tea. He had a very long, broad, silky-grey beard, that fell down right over his chest and was wider at the end than at the beginning. There was no hair at all on his head, but he had on a pair of big round spectacles. His eyes were not bright, but they were wonderfully kind and understanding. I noticed them in a moment, because I had not seen such kind and understanding eyes since my grandfather died. They looked as though they could see to the end of the world and understand the tiniest thing they met, and were sorry for all the people that were unhappy. They made me feel he must be almost holy (*not religious*).

He was one of the most learned men alive, but he was not too proud to talk to me although there were a lot of other people and I was so ignorant. And when we had been talking for some time I told him about the convent and the spiritualist meetings, and that I felt worried be-cause everything seemed so difficult to believe in, and everybody quarrelled so much about their beliefs. But

*Prince Peter Kropotkin.

he said that I need not worry, and that all little people needed to believe in was kindness and pity and love (just ordinary love for one another, not perfect love or anything complicated), and that our whole duty was to do what little good we could in the world as we passed through it, and to try to understand as much as possible of the wonders that surround us, and help others to understand them. He said it was ridiculous to imagine that a God who could create such a mighty and wonderful universe would be so petty as to care whether we crossed ourselves with two fingers or with three, or whether we ate fish or meat on Fridays, or what sort of church we went to, or what sort of prayers we said, or that He would wish to punish us for doing or not doing any of those things at all, so long as we had done our best so far as we could understand. He said we could quite safely go upon our way doing what we felt to be right without worrying about the consequences to ourselves hereafter.

He said that in Russia there had once been a great saint who taught the people how to live and had such a wonderful effect upon them that all the other saints in the neighbourhood were offended and the religious people said that he was anti-Christ. He didn't teach them about the proper way to be saved; all he said was, "Love one another." And because he was so good and gentle and because they loved and honoured him so much they did what he told them and lived in peace and were very happy. And later, when he was very old and when death was near, he retired with one or two disciples to the top of a mountain to die in peace, but great multitudes of the people followed him even there. And in order not to disappoint them he told his disciples to carry him out to them. And he was just able to lift his hand and bless them and whisper, "Children, love one another!" And they fell on their knees before him and swore to do his bidding. And the country all round the mountain was like paradise because the people were so well-behaved and never quarrelled or fought, or stole from one another or were cruel, because they loved one another. And God was pleased. And when the saint was safely dead and buried the other saints and religious people forgave him.

The learned gentleman said that the saint's lesson was the greatest lesson, and when once we had learnt it we should be happy and everything else would be made clear to us.

I said, "Thank you very much." And when afterwards I thought about what he had said, it seemed true and easy to understand and believe in. And I was glad because I thought I should not have to waste my time in worrying any more.

For I was growing a big girl, and there were so many things I had to learn and think about.

About the Author

Juliet M. Soskice was the young sister of Ford Madox Ford. Dante Gabriel and William Michael Rossetti were her uncles. Christina Rossetti was an aunt. The great pre-Raphaelite painter Ford Madox Brown was her grandfather. Mrs. Soskice is best known for her Russian translations. Her remarkable translations include Nikolai A. Nekrasov's "The Poet of the People's Sorrow" and Vikenti V. Veresaev's "The Sisters."